D1621803

Plate 2: The 9.10 Paddington to Birkenhead express is pictured near Loudwater, on 18th March 1957, headed by 'King' class locomotive No. 6016 *King John* of Old Oak Common Depot.

J. D. Edwards

THE GREAT WESTERN REMEMBERED

J. S. Whiteley and G. W. Morrison

Oxford Publishing Co.

Plate 3: A Great Western classic photograph taken at Flax Bourton, which is between Bristol and Bridgwater, of 'Star' class 4-6-0 No. 4014 *Knight of the Bath*, at the head of a Wolverhampton (Low Level) to Paignton express in 1939.

C. R. L. Coles

Copyright © 1985 J. S. Whiteley, G. W. Morrison and Oxford Publishing Co.

ISBN 0-86093-204-4

All rights reserved. No part of this book may be reproduced or transmitted in any form or by any means, electronic or mechanical, including photocopying, recording or any information storage and retrieval system, without permission in writing from the Publisher.

Typesetting by:
Aquarius Typesetting Services, New Milton, Hants.

Printed in Great Britain by:
Biddles Ltd., Guildford.

Published by:
Oxford Publishing Co.
Link House
West Street
POOLE, Dorset

Contents

Introduction

The Great Western Remembered is the fourth volume in a series, and is a companion volume to *The LMS Remembered, The LNER Remembered,* and *The Southern Remembered,* published in 1979 and 1980. It has been compiled on the same basis as the others by giving a photographic record of the company from the Grouping on 1st January 1923.

The Great Western Railway, of course, differed from the other companies as it was 1833 when it was planned in Bristol, and of the Big Four at the time of the Grouping, the Great Western took over eighteen comparatively small railway companies, the handing over taking a two year period. This resulted in the GWR inheriting a wide variety of small motive power. A large proportion of the locomotives which were inherited were already quite old, and the GWR was quick to sort out the motley collection of the older classes, by scrapping many, but also rebuilding others with standard Great Western features.

The Great Western always had an air of superiority, which tended to divide enthusiasts into those who worshipped it, and those who hated it, but if one looks at it dispassionately, it had good reasons for its attitude. Churchward had built what must be some of the finest express passenger locomotives ever to run in this country in the 'Saints' and the 'Stars', many of which put in fifty years service without any major modifications, and were still to be seen on express passenger work right up to their withdrawal. The same can also be said for the 2800 class 2-8-0s. The Collett era was really an extension of the firm basis set by Churchward, and so the outward appearance of GWR locomotives changed little over fifty years.

The GWR was always very publicity conscious, making much of the first-claimed 100m.p.h., with *City of Truro's* epic descent of Wellington Bank and the introduction of the first Pacific locomotive in this country in the shape of *The Great Bear*, which, as a locomotive, could hardly be considered a success, but certainly could as far as a publicity exercise was concerned. The various locomotive exchanges in the mid-1920s, when the 'Castles' demonstrated their superiority over LMS and LNER express locomotives, was also exploited to the full by the GWR Publicity Department.

From 1930 onwards, there were no major changes on the motive power side, the designs then in existence being basically sound enough to last until the end of steam, and the limelight then tended to be on the LMS and LNER who were both running their streamlined trains just prior to World War II. In spite of its deep-rooted steam traditions, the Western Region of British Rail was the first to eliminate steam from its main line operations, and indeed continued their forward-looking approach with the introduction of Inter-City 125 units.

The photographs selected for this book have been chosen to try and portray a balanced picture of the Great Western from 1923 onwards, and whilst most have not been published before, we felt that no Great Western album would be complete without a few of the late Maurice Earley classics. To all the other photographers who have put their collections at our disposal, we extend our thanks, and hope that Great Western enthusiasts will obtain as much pleasure from the book, as we have had in its compilation.

G. W. Morrison
October 1984

The Churchward Era

George Jackson Churchward was appointed Locomotive, Carriage and Wagon Superintendent of the Great Western Railway in 1902, succeeding William Dean, and so began the most significant period of locomotive design for the Great Western Railway, until his retirement in 1921.

His achievements in standardisation of design were never matched until the latter 1930s, when Sir William Stanier standardised designs for the LMS, followed by H. G. Ivatt and ultimately R. A. Riddles for British Railways.

Such was the excellence of his basic and rugged locomotives, that many lasted almost to the end of steam on British Railways, in some cases putting in over fifty years of service, and most without any major modifications.

The 2900 class 4-6-0 'Saints'

The prototype No. 100, later named *William Dean*, emerged from Swindon Works in 1902. The appearance of the locomotive caused quite a stir at the time, as it had none of the traditional lines of the period.

There were 77 of these magnificent locomotives constructed between 1902 and 1913, thirteen of them being built as 4-4-2s. These were all converted to 4-6-0s between April 1912 and January 1913. Few major alterations occurred throughout their working lives except for No. 2935 *Caynham Court*, which was fitted with rotary cam poppet valve gear and new cylinders in May 1931. No. 2925 *Saint Martin* was reconstructed with 6ft. driving wheels and larger cab in 1924, and became the prototype for the famous 'Hall' class, being renumbered 4900 and lasting in service until 1959. The first 'Saint' was withdrawn in 1931 and the last, No. 2920 *Saint David*, in 1953. Forty seven survived to enter service with British Railways in January 1948.

Plate 4 (left): Top link work for 'Saint' No. 2953 *Titley Court*, as it passes Chipping Sodbury on 30th June 1925, with an 'up' Bristol to Paddington express. When this photograph was taken, outside steam pipes had not been fitted, neither had whistle shields, which were added to the class from 1925. Comparison with *Plate 5* shows the extended safety-valve bonnet which was shortened after 1927.

H. G. W. Household

Plate 5 (below): After 39 years of service, 'Saint' No. 2951 *Tawstock Court* is seen at Gloucester Shed on 22nd June 1952, the month in which it was withdrawn from service. It was the first locomotive in the last batch of five to be constructed in 1913, and was one of the 33 members of the class to be fitted with a speedometer after 1937. Interchange of boilers with the 'Granges' took place after 1939, resulting in locomotives running with the smaller type of chimney, as is seen in this photograph.

L. Elsey

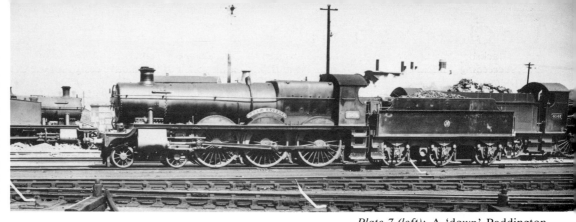

Plate 6 (right): A portrait of 'Saint' No. 2905 *Lady Macbeth* taken at Bristol (Bath Road) Shed 5th June 1938. This was one of the nineteen members of the class which had the older platforms with square 'drop ends'. After November 1930, the majority of the class was fitted with new front ends, which were given an estimated life of 25 years. No. 2905 was one of the class so fitted, which is indicated by the outside steam pipes. The locomotive is running in the 1934 livery with the circular totem of the letters GWR.

J. P. Wilson

Plate 7 (left): A 'down' Paddington to Swansea express is pictured near Burnham Beaches, on 25th April 1925, headed by 'Saint' No. 2907 *Lady Disdain*. Most of the early withdrawals from 1931 onwards tended, with a few exceptions, to be the locomotives which were not fitted with the new front ends. No. 2907 *Lady Disdain* was one of them, being withdrawn as early as 1933 after 27 years service.

H. G. W. Household

Plate 8 (below): On 10th July 1925, 'Saint' No. 2950 *Taplow Court* makes a splendid sight as it heads a 'down' Paddington to Swansea express on to the water troughs between Sodbury Tunnel and Chipping Sodbury Station.

H. G. W. Household

The 2800 class 2-8-0s

The prototype of this famous class, No. 97, appeared as early as June 1903. It was designed with many of the improvements incorporated in the second 'Saint', No. 98, and had the same type of boiler.

These locomotives have the distinction of being the first 2-8-0s in this country, and must surely rank as one of the most successful heavy freight locomotives ever to be built in the British Isles. The class ultimately consisted of 167 locomotives, 84 being built between 1903 and 1919, followed by a gap of 20 years before C. B. Collett constructed the remainder between 1938 and 1942. There were very few alterations to the original design except for side window cabs, outside steam pipes, and modified framing. Twenty members of the class were converted to oil burning between October 1945 and September 1947, but by January 1950 all had been reconverted to coal.

One member of the class, No. 2804, visited Scotland for trials on the Glenfarg Incline in January 1921, and No. 3803 took part in the 'Locomotive Exchange' trials of 1948. The prototype, which became No. 2800, is recorded as having covered 1,319,831 miles during its 55 years of service, and was in fact the first to be withdrawn in 1958. The last to be withdrawn was No. 3836, which was taken out of traffic in 1965.

Plate 9 (above): Having probably just received its last major overhaul, 2-8-0 No. 2861, built in June 1918, stands outside Swindon Works on 2nd September 1956, ready to resume duties from its home depot of Newport.

Gavin Morrison

Plate 10 (above): The class was not often used on passenger duties, but occasionally they appeared during busy summer Saturdays in Devon and Cornwall. In this photograph, No. 2836 is seen in August 1959 heading an 'up' empty stock train, south of Oxford.

J. D. Edwards

Plate 11 (left): No. 2830, which was the last of lot number 160 to be built in 1907, is seen after 45 years service working very hard through Leamington Spa on 25th September 1952, with a heavy 'up' freight.

B. Morrison

Plate 12 (right): No. 3805 has just received a major overhaul at Swindon and is seen at Westbury Shed on 1st October 1961, looking very smart in its unlined black livery. The side window cab can be clearly seen in this picture compared with *Plate 9.* The Collett-built locomotives were known as the 2884 class.

Gavin Morrison

Plate 13 (below): The gentleman taking the sea air along the wall at Teignmouth seems unimpressed by this fine sight of No. 3838 heading a 'down' freight towards Newton Abbot on 2nd October 1959.

L. Elsey

The Prairie Tanks
The 3100, 3150, 5100, 5101, 6100 and 8100 class 2-6-2Ts

Plate 14 (above): No. 3100, rebuilt from No. 3173 in December 1938, awaits scrapping on 8th September 1957, at Swindon Works. These five rebuilds were originally intended for banking duties, but by 1950 were regularly being used for suburban trains around Wolverhampton, Newport and Tondu.

Gavin Morrison

Three hundred and six of these fine 2-6-2Ts were constructed over the lengthy period from 1903 to 1949.

The prototype, No. 99, had an interesting career. It appeared in 1903, and was thoroughly tested for over a year by Churchward before any further locomotives were constructed. No. 99 later became No. 3100, in December 1912. It ran as such until April 1929 when it became No. 5100. The side tanks were altered at this time from straight-topped to the sloping pattern, and it also received a long-cone boiler in 1910.

A start on rebuilding the first forty locomotives (Nos. 3100, 3111-3149), built between 1903 and 1906, was made in 1938, but the war interrupted the programme after only ten had been altered. The prototype, No. 99, finally became the first of the 8100 class in September 1938 when it was rebuilt using the original frames but having new front ends fitted, a boiler with high pressure, and 5ft. 6in. diameter coupled wheels.

The 1938 batch of rebuilds, Nos. 3100-3104 were also interrupted by the war, these being from the larger boilered 3150 series.

Some of the locomotives were constructed in 1949 so had as little as twelve years service. The vast majority of the class operated in the Wolverhampton/Birmingham areas, with the exception of the 6100s, which were almost exclusively used on the London suburban services.

Plate 15 (below): No. 3102, with a newly-painted smokebox, is seen shunting in the yards of Wolverhampton, prior to leaving with a freight for Wrexham. The locomotive, which was a rebuild of No. 3181 in May 1939, was allocated to Wolverhampton (Stafford Road) Shed when this picture was taken on 20th July 1954.   *B. Morrison*

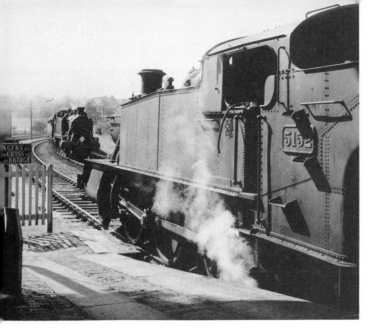

Plate 16 (above): A 5101 class locomotive, No. 5152, prepares to leave Chipping Norton on 14th September 1963, as No. 6111 arrives with a Railway Enthusiasts' Club special.

J. R. P. Hunt

Plate 19 (below): A fine study of one of the original batch of Class 5100 locomotives built in 1906. No. 5132 is leaving Exeter St. David's on 5th June 1949, with a local train for Torquay. Note the absence of outside steam pipes; only six out of the batch of forty received them from 1943 onwards. This locomotive put in forty five years service, compared with twelve for some of the 5101 class.

J. P. Wilson

Plate 17 (above): Another 5101 class locomotive, built in November 1929, No. 5103, is ready to leave Ruabon on 9th August 1956 with the 17.04 local train to Llangollen.

B. Morrison

Plate 18 (left): A portrait of one of the post-war batch of Class 5101, No. 4144, is seen in the lined Brunswick green livery of British Railways at Cardiff (Canton) Depot on 3rd June 1962. This locomotive is one of several members of the class which have been preserved.

Gavin Morrison

Plate 21 (above): 6100 class No. 6132 looks very smart, on 14th October 1962, at Southall Shed in its unlined green livery with small emblem.

Gavin Morrison

Plate 20 (above): One of the seventy 6100 class loco-motives, No. 6103, built with 225lb. boiler pressure, is approaching High Wycombe on a local train from Banbury on 6th June 1953. The class was specifically-built for London suburban work, and all operated in the division until 1954. The introduction of diesel multiple units in 1960 saw their rapid demise.

B. Morrison

Plate 22 (below): No. 8100 was in fact the third 5100 class to be rebuilt, in September 1938. It went to Leamington after re-building, where it is seen on 17th June 1951, alongside railcar No. W22, built in 1940 with an AEC engine. For the history of No. 8100 (which contained the frames of the 1903 prototype 2-6-2T) reference should be made to the introductory notes on the Prairie tanks on Page 10.

B. Morrison

The 3800 class 4-4-0 'Counties'

Plate 23 (above): An official works photograph of No. 3821 *County of Bedford*, which was the first of the final batch of ten, and which varied from the original thirty in that they had curved drop-ends to the footplating (*compare Plates 24 & 25 below*). These locomotives were the only outside-cylindered 4-4-0s built by the Great Western, and the reason for their construction, in view of the success of the 'Saints' and the rebuilding of some of the Dean 4-4-0s, is rather obscure. They were used initially on the Shrewsbury to Hereford route where the LNWR objected to the use of 4-6-0s. They were extremely rough-riding locomotives and probably the least successful of the Churchward engines. They were soon demoted to secondary work and withdrawn in the early 1930s.

OPC/British Rail Collection

Plate 24 (above): No. 3825 *County of Denbigh* is seen on express passenger duties on 18th July 1926, near Cheletenham (Racecourse) Station, with a Paignton to Wolverhampton train, which consists of quite a variety of coaching stock.

H. G. W. Household

Plate 25 (above): One of the members of the second batch of ten built in 1906, all of which were named after Irish counties, is seen on 9th July 1924, near Hatherley Junction, Cheltenham, hauling a Penzance to Wolverhampton express. The locomotive is No. 3804 *County Dublin*, and is paired to the tender off *The Great Bear* which it received in June 1924. Two other members of the class ran with this tender, possibly in an attempt to stabilise them.

H. G. W. Household

The 2221 class 4-4-2 'County' Tanks

Plate 26 (right): These locomotives were basically tank versions of the 'County' 3800 class, but had a smaller boiler. Thirty of the class were built between 1905 and 1912. They were primarily used on outer London suburban services, hence the large 6ft. 8½in. coupled wheels. They were rapidly withdrawn in the early 1930s, after the introduction of the 6100 class. No. 2235 is seen at Oxford on 1st July 1934.

R. C. Riley Collection

The 4000 class 4-6-0 'Stars'

Based upon the experience gained from the three 'De Glehn' Compound Atlantics and his two cylinder 4-6-0 'Saints', Churchward produced, in 1906, the first of what many have regarded as his finest class of locomotive, the 'Stars'. No. 40 (later numbered 4000) emerged as a 4-4-2 and ran in this condition, together with other differences from the rest of the class, until November 1909, when it became a 4-6-0. Seventy three of these locomotives, including No. 40, were built by 1923, thirty nine surviving to enter service with British Railways. They altered little in appearance during their existence, except for the addition of outside steam pipes. Right up to the end, they could be seen working heavy express trains, some members covering over two million miles during their life. Between 1925 and 1929, five were rebuilt as 'Castles', followed in 1940 by a further ten (Nos. 4063-72) which became 'Castles' Nos. 5083-92. After 1938, most of the class received 4,000 gallon high-sided tenders.

Plate 27 (above): On 25th April 1925, No. 4015 *Knight of St. John* is pictured near Burnham Beeches, Buckinghamshire, at the head of the 2.30p.m. Cheltenham to Paddington express, which was only allowed 75 minutes for the 77 miles from Swindon to Paddington.

H. G. W. Household

Plate 28 (right): No. 4034 *Queen Adelaide*, built in November 1910, passes along the sea wall near Teignmouth with the 'down' 'Cornish Riviera' express on 24th April 1924.

H. G. W. Household

Plate 29 (below): A 'Star', at the peak of its career, hauling the heavy 'up' 'Cornish Riviera' express. The locomotive is No. 4042 *Prince Albert*, built in May 1913, and lasting over 38 years. It is seen between Teignmouth and Dawlish, on 24th April 1924.

H. G. W. Household

Plate 30 (right): On 24th September 1955, the Talyllyn Railway Preservation Society's annual special makes a fine sight as it nears the top of Hatton Bank, headed by No. 4061 *Glastonbury Abbey* with its number specially painted on the buffer beam for the occasion by Tyseley Shed. The locomotive is fitted with the elbow steam pipes.

R. C. Riley

Plate 31 (below): The external condition of No. 4056 *Princess Margaret* is in sharp contrast to *Plate 32.* The locomotive is heading a 'down' express past Southall, on 10th August 1957, with the number painted on the buffer beam for working an enthusiasts' special.

R. C. Riley

Plate 32 (below): No. 4056 *Princess Margaret* was the last of the class to be withdrawn, in October 1957. Built in July 1914, it had the elbow-type outside steam pipes added in August 1949, and it also has the 4,000 gallon tender. Two members of the class, Nos. 4059 and 4062, ran with the Hawksworth flat-sided tenders, whilst in 1936, Nos. 4045 and 4022 had *The Great Bear* tender. No. 4056 spent its later days at Bristol (Bath Road) Shed where it is seen on 9th March 1952.

L. Elsey

Plate 33 (left): The last of the 4400 class, No. 4410, is seen working the Princetown branch at Dousland on 2nd July 1955. These locomotives worked this branch for many years, and the sharp curves and steep gradients caused considerable flange wear on the coupled wheels; oiling devices were tried without success. They were also to be found on other Cornish branch lines, in addition to the Porthcawl and Much Wenlock lines.

R. C. Riley

Plate 34 (below): A lovely photograph, taken on 7th July 1956, of No. 5508 when stationed at Westbury, ready to leave Bristol (Temple Meads) with the 10.17 working to Frome. The loco-motive is in the unlined black livery which was the original livery chosen for the class by British Railways.

J. P. Wilson

The 4400, 4500 and 4575 class 2-6-2Ts

These fine little 2-6-2Ts were very similar. The 4400s had 4ft. 1½in. coupled wheels, but the 4500 and 4575 classes had the diameter of the coupled wheels increased to 4ft. 7½in., to give them a 60m.p.h. capability. Eleven of the 4400s were built in 1905, the first one, No. 4400, being built at Swindon and the rest at Wolverhampton. Fifty five of the Class 4500 were built between 1906 and 1915, and as was so often the case with Churchward's successful designs, a gap of nine years elapsed before a further 120 were constructed between 1924 and 1929. The last 100 engines had larger side tanks with 1,300 gallons capacity, compared to 1,000 gallons for the earlier locomotives. All entered service with British Rail. Nos. 4500-29 were originally built without outside steam pipes which were added from 1929 onwards. Auto-apparatus was fitted to fifteen members of the class between August and November 1953 for working in the South Wales valleys.

No. 111 4-6-2 *The Great Bear*.

Much has been written over the years about this locomotive. It appears that Churchward was instructed by the company's Directors, contrary to his own wishes, to build, as cheaply as possible, the largest locomotive in the country.

The locomotive was presented to the Directors at Paddington in January 1908, and immediately received considerable interest. As a publicity exercise, the locomotive was a huge success being the only British Pacific for fourteen years. Operationally, it was a different story; its size and weight restricted its use to the Paddington to Bristol line, with very few wanderings. It was restricted to 65m.p.h., and caused constant worry to the permanent way engineering department. When costly repairs were due in January 1924, Churchward grasped the opportunity to rebuild the locomotive as a 'Castle', which emerged as No. 111, but renamed *Viscount Churchill*. The eight-wheeled tender lasted a further twelve years in traffic and ran with many different classes.

Plate 35 (above): An official photograph of the locomotive.
OPC/British Rail Collection

Plate 36 (right): About one year after rebuilding from *The Great Bear*, it is seen as 'Castle' class locomotive No. 111, now *Viscount Churchill*, with a 3,500 gallon tender, at Slough on 25th April 1925.

H. G. W. Household

Plate 37 (below): This is, no doubt, one of the publicity photographs taken of No. 111, showing its massive proportions. The total length of engine and tender over buffers was 71ft. 2¼in., almost 7ft. longer than a 'Star', and at 142 tons 15 cwt. in full working order, about 28 tons more than a 'Star'. Not only was the engine restricted to the Bristol line, but it was banned from using platform 1 at Paddington. It was always allocated to Old Oak Common.

OPC/British Rail Collection

The 4200 and 5205 class 2-8-0Ts

The increase in mineral traffic in South Wales in the early 1900s meant that there was a need for a tank version of the famous 2800 class. A 2-8-2T design was considered but rejected mainly on the length of the wheelbase, bearing in mind the environment in which the locomotives would work, so a 2-8-0T prototype appeared in 1910 as No. 4201. Fourteen months elapsed before any more were built, there being little variation between No. 4201 and the others, except for an increase of the coal bunker capacity and the fitting of top feed. The 5205 class, introduced in 1923, had outside steam pipes and an increased cylinder diameter to 19in., which increased the tractive effort. Fourteen of the 4201 series were rebuilt as 2-8-2Ts, to increase their operating capabilites, whilst Nos. 5255-5294 were also converted. Nos. 5275-5294 never entered traffic as 2-8-0Ts and were stored at Swindon prior to conversion. Due to wartime demands, a further batch of ten was built as late as 1940, being numbered 5255-5264.

Plate 38 (above): One of the last batch to be built in 1940, and in fact the second 2-8-0T to be numbered 5261, the original becoming 2-8-2T No. 7226, is seen in ex-works condition in the standard British Railways livery of unlined black on 3rd June 1962, at Cardiff (Canton) Shed. Note the raised running plate above the cylinders, compared with No. 4289 in *Plate 39.*

Gavin Morrison

Plate 39 (below): On 5th February 1953, No. 4289 is pictured near Ely, west of Cardiff on a 'down' freight. Two hundred and five of these locomotives were built, including the ones converted to 2-8-2T, all entering service with British Railways, the last one, No. 5235, being withdrawn in 1965.

S. Rickard

The 4300 class 2-6-0s

No prototype was considered necessary for these extremely successful Moguls, of which 324 were built between 1911 and 1932. They were, in fact, a tender version of the 3150 class 2-6-2Ts, and the first new GWR locomotives to be built with top feed. The second batch, built in 1913, Nos. 4321-40, had the frames lengthened by 9in., as did the remainder, but this batch also had enlarged cabs, similar to the 3800 'County' class.

Eighty eight of the 4300 series and twelve of the 8300 series were withdrawn between 1936 and 1939 and some parts, particularly the wheels and motion, were used on the 'Granges' and 'Manors'. From 1928, sixty five locomotives had their weight distribution altered and they became the 8300 class, but they reverted to their original condition in 1944 and to their original numbers. From No. 6362 onwards, outside steam pipes were fitted new, many of the earlier locomotives being modified from 1928 onwards. The first locomotive was withdrawn in 1936 and the last in 1965. One locomotive, No. 6320, was converted to oil burning in March 1947, reverting back to coal in August 1949.

Plate 40 (above): No. 6323 is seen on Bristol (Bath Road) Shed. This photograph was taken on 5th June 1938, before the outside steam pipes were added ten years later. Note the automatic tablet catcher on the tender. Seven locomotives ran with tablet catchers at various times and were used on the Minehead and Barnstaple branches.

J. P. Wilson

Plate 41 (below): A very dirty No. 5381, which became No. 8381 in 1928 and reverted back in 1944, is seen on a very lengthy freight passing Beaconsfield, en route to London, on 13th August 1956.

Gavin Morrison

Plate 42 (left): No. 6352 enters Lydney Junction on 19th May 1958, at the head of the 12.40p.m. slow passenger train from Carmarthen to Cheltenham.

J. D. Edwards

Plate 43 (below): The 1932 batch, numbered 9300-9319, was built with the same weight distribution as the modified 8300 locomotives. Between 1956 and 1959, they were altered back to the 5300 weight specification and became Nos. 7322-7341. No. 7324 is seen at Banbury Shed on 18th May 1958 (note the side window cab).

F. J. Bullock

Plate 44 (below): An unusual meeting at Oxford of the Midland Compound No. 1000 and Mogul No. 7317. This picture was taken during a loco-motive change on a railtour from Nottingham to Eastleigh on 11th September 1960, returning via the Midland & South Western Joint Railway. The ex-works Mogul, in unlined green livery, gave a spirited performance, reaching the upper seventies down the bank through Winchester. Other locations where these two classes could have been regularly seen together would have been Chester, Birkenhead and, possibly, Crewe.

Gavin Morrison

The 4700 class 2-8-0s

The performance of *The Great Bear* on fitted freight work had been partly successful, and a request from the traffic department for a locomotive to work heavy fast vacuum-fitted freights led Churchward to produce the 4700 class. Only nine were built, No. 4700 appearing in 1919 with a standard No. 1 boiler. The remainder of the class were constructed with the new No. 7 boiler and with outside steam pipes, No. 4700 being altered accordingly. From 1932, the 3,500 gallon tenders were replaced with the 4,000 gallon type. Generally speaking, these very successful locomotives changed little in appearance. They spent most of their lives working at night on express freights between London, Wolverhampton and Plymouth. Their weight and size restricted their route availability, but in their latter years they were frequently seen, in the summer, working expresses between Paddington and Devon, and maintaining schedules on all but the fastest workings. They were the last of Churchward's famous designs, and it is a pity that one was not preserved.

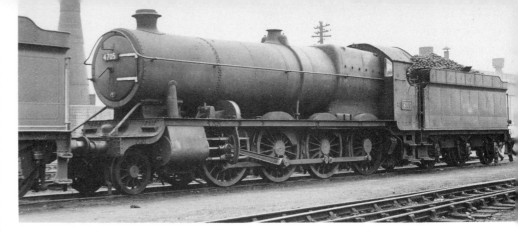

Plate 45 (above): No. 4705 is seen on Southall Shed on 28th April 1963, at the end of its working life of forty years. This locomotive achieved the highest mileage for a member of the class of 1,656,564 miles.

Gavin Morrison

Plate 46 (right): In 1953, the 5.14p.m. Paddington to Weston-super-Mare fast train is pictured crossing from the main to relief line at Twyford East box, and is headed by No. 4708.

M. W. Earley

Plate 47 (below): On express passenger duty, No. 4706 passes through the centre road at Newbury at the head of a Paddington to Paignton train on 29th August 1959.

L. Elsey

The Collett Era

C. B. Collett was appointed Chief Mechanical Engineer of the Great Western Railway in 1922. During his twenty years in this capacity, he appreciated the excellence of G. J. Churchward's designs and concentrated much of his efforts in developing and expanding them. This policy resulted in the building of what are probably the most famous of Great Western Locomotives, namely the 'Castles' and 'Kings', which became the mainstay of Great Western express motive power through the glamorous pre-war years, and indeed virtually to the end of steam on the Western Region. His pannier tanks were equally famous if much less glamorous and his forward thinking attitude produced the streamlined diesel railcars, as early as 1934. He retired in 1941.

The 4073 class 4-6-0 'Castles'

Plate 48 (above): No. 5054 *Earl of Ducie* is seen on Carmarthen Shed on 9th September 1962, just after receiving what was probably its last major repair at Swindon.

Gavin Morrison

Plate 49 (below): No. 5017 *The Gloucestershire Regiment 28th, 61st* seen on 11th May 1956, at Gloucester Station. This locomotive was originally named *St. Donats Castle,* the alteration being made in April 1954. The locomotive covered 1,598,851 miles in its thirty years of service.

W. Potter, D. Cobbe Collection

One hundred & seventy one of these famous locomotives were built (including rebuilds) between 1923 and 1950. By the Grouping, the weight of trains dictated that something more powerful than a 'Star' was needed, but it had to be within the 20 ton axle load permitted by the Civil Engineer. Collett followed Churchward's cautious approach to the introduction of new locomotives, in that No. 4073 operated for six months on 'Star' diagrams before the second engine was completed. No. 4073 *Caerphilly Castle* was exhibited in 1924 close to the LNER *Flying Scotsman* at the British Empire Exhibition at Wembley, the GWR stating that it was the most powerful passenger locomotive in the country. This resulted in the comparative trials between the two types on each other's main lines, the 'Castle' substantiating the claims about it with ease. No. 5000 *Launceston Castle* also ran trials between Euston and Carlisle. Nos. 4000/09/16/32/37 and 5083-5092 were rebuilt from 'Stars', and there was little alteration to the appearance of the class until No. 7018 *Drysllwyn Castle* appeared with a double chimney in May 1956, and with three-row superheater. The next locomotive modified was No. 4090 having four-row superheater. Sixty five locomotives were so modified, and in this condition achieved some of their finest performances. The 3,500 gallon tenders were replaced by ones of 4,000 gallon capacity, Hawksworth flat-sided tenders being constructed for the final batch, from No. 7008 onwards, and these were freely interchanged. Five locomotives were converted to oil burning in 1946 and 1947 but were changed back by the end of 1948. The 'Castles' must be unique in British express locomotive design in that they were built over a period of 28 years with only minor alterations, and remained on top link work for 38 years.

Plate 50 (above): A pre-war picture, taken on 22nd July 1937, of No. 5042 *Winchester Castle* approaching Swindon on a 'down' Paddington to Bristol and Weston-super-Mare express. Built in July 1935, the locomotive saw thirty years of service covering 1,339,221 miles.
J. P. Wilson

Plate 51 (below): The real No. 4082 *Windsor Castle* is seen on Royal Train duties from Weymouth to London as it passes Reading (West) Station in June 1938, fully decorated, and with the magnificent LNWR coaches. This locomotive took part in the Stockton & Darlington Centenary celebrations in 1925, and was unique in having the honour of being driven from Swindon Works to the station by His Majesty King George V with Queen Mary also on the footplate. It carried a plaque to commemorate the event. It was under repair in February 1952, and was therefore not available to haul the funeral train of King George VI, so the name, numbers and plaque were transferred to No. 7013 *Bristol Castle*. They were never replaced on the real No. 4082.
M. W. Earley

Plate 52 (left): The down 'Torbay Express' leaves Exeter St. David's on 2nd June 1957, headed by an immaculate 'Castle', No. 5059 *Earl St. Aldwyn.*

F. J. Bullock

Plate 53 (below): One of the late M. W. Earley classic photographs of 'Castles' shows No. 5035 *Coity Castle* heading the 11.15a.m. ex-Paddington (Sunday) fast train for Weston-super-Mare and Taunton. It is seen in November 1951 passing Tilehurst. The River Thames can be seen in the background. The smart external condition was so typical of the way that Old Oak Common kept the express locomotives at this time.

M. W. Earley

Plate 54 (right): The 1.45p.m. Paddington to Hereford train passes the outskirts of Oxford at North Junction, headed by one of the immaculate Worcester 'Castles', No. 7005 *Sir Edward Elgar*, on 22nd October 1957. This locomotive was originally named *Lamphey Castle*. Only the leading four or five coaches would work forward to Hereford from Worcester.

J. D. Edwards

Plate 55 (left): On 4th March 1958, No. 5005 *Manorbier Castle* is seen at speed on the Swindon Test Plant rollers.

J. D. Edwards

Plate 56 (right): 'Castle' class locomotive No. 5056, *Earl of Powis*, of Old Oak Common Shed, hauls the 2.10p.m. express from Paddington to Birkenhead and is pictured near Seer Green. This locomotive was originally named *Ogmore Castle* but was renamed in September 1937.

J. D. Edwards

Plate 57 (above left): No. 5086 *Viscount Horne* enters Bristol (Temple Meads) on 4th June 1949, with a Penzance to Wolverhampton express. This was one of the ten 'Castles' which were rebuilt from 'Stars' between 1937 and 1940. The rolling stock looks to be nearly as dirty as the locomotive.

J. P. Wilson

Plate 58 (below left): Probably the most spectacular locations on the Great Western Railway for photography, are the tunnels between Dawlish and Teignmouth. Unfortunately the photographer was not blessed with a clean locomotive, but in spite of the external condition, No. 5058 *Earl of Clancarty* makes a fine sight, as it heads a 'down' express on 5th June 1949, at Horse Cove.

J. P. Wilson

Plate 59 (above): In March 1935, in keeping with the fashion of the late 1930s, No. 5005 *Manorbier Castle* was partially streamlined. These features were gradually removed from the end of 1935 onwards, until by 1946 the only evidence left was the snifting valve. It is seen at Westbourne Park on an 'up' express on 14th July 1937.

J. P. Wilson

Plate 60 (below): A Birkenhead to Bournemouth express, formed of Southern stock, leaves Leamington Spa headed by No. 5053 *Earl Cairns* on 19th February 1949.

J. P. Wilson

Plate 61 (left): The clock on the side of the signal box at the west end of Swindon Station indicated the time as 9.50a.m. as an unidentified 'up' express, headed by 'Castle' No. 5057 *Earl Waldergrave*, passes through on the fast line on 13th June 1959.

J. D. Edwards

Plate 62 (right): The 'down' 'Cambrian Coast Express' rushes through Beaconsfield on 20th September 1958, headed by No. 7013 *Bristol Castle*. This was, in fact, the original No. 4082 *Windsor Castle*, built in April 1924, but it changed identities in 1952 when it was not available to work the funeral train of King George VI *(See Plate 51).* The locomotive is in its final condition with double blastpipe and chimney, and final pattern outside steam pipes with larger radius curves to allow clearance for the bulky four-row superheater header inside.

Gavin Morrison

Plate 63 (below): One of the well-kept Wolverhampton (Stafford Road) 'Castles', No. 5010 *Restormel Castle*, is seen approaching High Wycombe (Middle) signal box, with an 'up' morning express from Wolverhampton to Paddington on 11th April 1957.

J. D. Edwards

Plate 64 (right): On 29th April 1958, the 4.45p.m. Paddington to Hereford train is seen drifting into Oxford, past the cemetery, headed by a superbly-groomed Worcester 'Castle', No. 7005 *Sir Edward Elgar*. It is noticeable that even the buffer heads have been polished.

J. D. Edwards

Plate 65 (below): The last express passenger engine to be built by the Great Western at Swindon was 'Castle' class No. 7007, appropriately named *Great Western*, which was the same name as the first locomotive built in 1846. On 21st March 1960, No. 7007 is pictured leaving Oxford with a 'down' express from Paddington to Worcester, where the locomotive spent the majority of its working life.

J. D. Edwards

Plate 66 (above): On 14th July 1958, the 'down' 'Torbay Express' is seen passing through the cutting at Teignmouth Quay, headed by No. 5034 *Corfe Castle* which was built in 1935 and withdrawn in September 1962, having covered 1,250,714 miles.

R. C. Riley

Plate 67 (above right): An immaculate No. 5021, *Whittington Castle*, overshadowed by a large gasometer, arrives at Newquay with an excursion from Exeter on 21st July 1954.

L. Elsey

Plate 68 (above): Another view of No. 5034 *Corfe Castle* with the 'up' 'Torbay Express' passing along the sea wall at Teignmouth. The locomotive had received a good cleaning during the three days that separate this picture, taken on 17th July 1958, and that in *Plate 66*.

R. C. Riley

Plate 69 (left): Landore Depot at Swansea have certainly spent some time cleaning 'Castle' No. 4099 *Kilgerren Castle*. It was photographed at Swansea (High Street) from the window of the 5.25p.m. departure for Carmarthen, and was ready to leave on the 5.30p.m. for Paddington on 17th May 1958.

J. D. Edwards

Plate 70 (above): On 18th April 1964, only ten months before withdrawal and looking well cared for and complete with nameplate, No. 7011 *Banbury Castle* enters Evesham with a Worcester to Paddington express. It was built in 1949 by British Railways under the direction of Hawksworth, and is running with one of his flat-sided tenders.

J. R. P. Hunt

Plate 71 (above): One of the 65 'Castles' fitted with four-row superheaters and double chimney, No. 7023 *Penrice Castle*, makes a spirited departure, on 7th June 1964, from Bath (Green Park) on a railtour. This was one of the very few, if not the only occasion when a 'Castle' visited the old Somerset & Dorset terminus.

Gavin Morrison

Plate 72 (left): Another of the class with a double chimney and, since preservation, one of the best-known 'Castles'. No. 7029 *Clun Castle* is seen outside Swindon Shed on 26th April 1964. Withdrawn in December 1965, it only had a life of fifteen years in normal service, but happily it is now regularly used on steam specials.

Gavin Morrison

Plate 73 (below): On 3rd June 1962, only one month before withdrawal, No. 5053 *Earl Cairns* is seen at the back of Cardiff (Canton) Shed fitted with a Hawksworth tender. It was originally named *Bishop's Castle*, but altered to *Earl Cairns* in August 1937. It covered 1,293,786 miles in its 26 years of service.

Gavin Morrison

Plate 74 (below): No. 5062 *Earl of Shaftesbury* is stored, complete with nameplate, at Cardiff (Canton), on 3rd June 1962, the locomotive having run its last revenue-earning trip, as it was officially withdrawn two months after this photograph was taken. It was originally named *Tenby Castle* and was renamed in November 1937. *Tenby Castle* became No. 7026 in 1949.

Gavin Morrison

The 4900 class 4-6-0 'Halls'

The 'Halls' became the 'maids of all work' on the Great Western from the latter 1920s until the end of steam.

The Churchward 4300 class Moguls had been giving excellent service, but the running department and the footplatemen tended to expect rather too much from them. Many years previous, Churchward had considered the 'Hall' design, but nothing happened until Collett put it into practice. The usual cautious approach, which had paid such handsome dividends so many times before, was again implemented. No. 2925 *Saint Martin* was selected in 1924 as the guinea pig, having the coupled wheels reduced in diameter from 6ft. 8½in. to 6ft., and also fitted with a side window cab. This locomotive, which was renumbered 4900, was tested with great success for nearly three years, when an initial order was then placed in 1928 for no less than eighty engines. There was little variance between No. 4900 and the production models, which had outside steam pipes and a raised boiler pitch. The first 42 locomotives were built with Churchward-type 3,500 gallon tenders, Nos. 4943-4957 then had the Collett type, and finally the remainder, with the odd exception, had the 4,000 gallon pattern. Two hundred and fifty nine of these locomotives were built up to 1943, when a further 71 modified locomotives were constructed by Hawksworth.

Eleven locomotives were converted to oil burning in 1946 and 1947, but all had been reconverted by March 1950.

All locomotives survived to enter service with British Railways, except No. 4911 *Bowden Hall*, which was destroyed by enemy action in April 1940. No. 4900 *Saint Martin* was the first to be withdrawn in 1959, with a total mileage for its career of 2,092,500 miles.

Plate 75 (above): On 25th July 1962, No. 6957 *Norcliffe Hall* pauses at Dainton Summit to pin down the brakes on this mixed freight, before descending the steep gradient to Totnes. This locomotive was one of the eleven 'Halls' converted to oil burning in April 1947, and carried the number 3952 after the conversion.
John Whiteley

Plate 76 (below): A superb night study of Cardiff Canton's No. 4956 *Plowden Hall*, as it waits for the road at Oxford on a fitted freight heading south, in the late evening of 8th August 1959.
J. D. Edwards

Plate 77 (above): Nottingham (Victoria) was the farthest north that Great Western locomotives ventured down the Great Central, except on very rare occasions, (see Plate 160). No. 5973 *Rolleston Hall*, built in May 1937, prepares to head south with a rake of southern stock on a return excursion to Poole, which it would probably work as far as Oxford.

J. P. Wilson

Plate 78 (below): A fine pre-war scene in 1938 at Reading (West) shows No. 5971 *Merevale Hall*, when only about a year old, heading an 'up' Weymouth express.

M. W. Earley

Plate 79 (left): No. 5967 *Bickmarsh Hall* is seen on Westbury Shed on 1st November 1961, fitted with a smaller diameter chimney, which some of the class carried after they had exchanged boilers from the later 'Modified Halls' during overhaul at Swindon. This locomotive was constructed in March 1937.

Gavin Morrison

Plate 80 (right): Another portrait taken at Westbury Shed, on 23rd April 1962, this time of No. 4920 *Dumbleton Hall*, obviously recently ex-works and, at this time, allocated to Plymouth (Laira). Happily this locomotive has been preserved and is currently being restored at the Dart Valley Railway.

Gavin Morrison

Plate 81 (left): 1st October 196 sees a well-groomed Exeter-allocated 'Hall', No. 5976 *Ashwicke Hall* on Bristol (St. Philip's Marsh) Depot attached to a Hawksworth 4,000 gallon tender. These tenders were constructed for the 'Modified Halls'.

Gavin Morrison

Plate 82 (above): The British Railways' lined black livery was extremely smart and No. 4908 *Broome Hall* shows it to advantage on 31st July 1956, as it leaves Par with an 'up' express on the stiff climb to Treverrin Tunnel.

L. Elsey

Plate 83 (below): A busy scene at Shrewsbury, as a commendably clean No. 4976 *Warfield Hall* leaves with a Hastings to Birkenhead express. An ex-LMS 8F, No. 48706, is seen alongside and No. 2933 *Bibury Court* awaits departure with the 16.50 train for Gobowen on 28th August 1952.

B. Morrison

Plate 84 (left): No. 6901 *Arley Hall* makes a smokey exit from Shrewsbury on 23rd June 1962, as it starts the long climb to Church Stretton with a freight, probably destined for South Wales.

John Whiteley

Plate 85 (right): A really dirty No. 6952 *Kimberley Hall*, built in 1963, makes a spectacular departure from Oxford on a Cowley to Birkenhead freight on 21st March 1960, and passes some new diesel multiple units.

J. D. Edwards

Plate 86 (left): On 27th August 1959, Llanelly-based 'Hall', No 5902 *Howick Hall* passes Oxford (North) Junction with an 'up' freight. The connection to the former LNWR line to Bletchley can be seen curving to the right, behind the leading wagons.

J. D. Edwards

Plate 87 (right): On 14th June 1958, the 4.18p.m. train from Swindon has just arrived at Didcot behind 'Hall' No. 4918 *Dartington Hall*, which appears to have recently visited the works. A 4300 class 2-6-0 No. 5397 is about to remove the empty carriage stock from the 2.42p.m. train from Paddington, in spite of the headlamp code indicating an express. The locomotive shed can be seen on the right, and this is now the headquarters of the Great Western Preservation Society.

J. D. Edwards

Plate 88 (above): On 30th September 1961, No. 5974 *Wallsworth Hall* of Westbury emerges from Bincombe Tunnel at Upwey Wishing Well Halt, as it descends rapidly down the line to Weymouth with a train from the Western Region.

Gavin Morrison

Plate 89 (right): On 23rd June 1962, a southbound parcels heads over the north/west joint route at Bayston Hill, just south of Shrewsbury, headed by No. 6934 *Beachamwell Hall*, fitted with a 'Modified Hall' boiler.

John Whiteley

The 6959 class 4-6-0 'Modified Halls'

Hawksworth produced seventy-one of these 'Modified Halls' between March 1944 and November 1950. The main differences between these and 'Halls' were three-row superheaters fitted to the standard No. 1 boilers, main plate frames were used throughout with a simple plate frame bogie, and new pattern cylinders were fitted. Several different experiments were carried out on locomotives during construction, resulting in some small variances in the class. No. 6974 was the first to have the new pattern Hawksworth 4,000 gallon straight-sided tender. Nos. 6959-6970 were built during the war without cabside windows, which were subsequently fitted between 1945 and 1948, and they also ran without nameplates for two or three years. No. 6962 was the first to be withdrawn in 1963, some of the class only having fifteen years of service.

Plate 90 (above left): No. 6994 *Baggrave Hall* is pictured well coaled up on 14th October 1962, on Southall Shed, with a Collett-type tender.

Gavin Morrison

Plate 93 (above right): No. 7920 *Coney Hall* has just arrived at Birmingham (Snow Hill) with a morning commuter train from Leamington Spa on 10th March 1964.

J. R. P. Hunt

Plate 91 (centre left): Tyseley Junction is the setting for this picture of No. 7918 *Rhose Wood Hall*, taking the Stratford-upon-Avon line with an evening commuter train from Birmingham (Snow Hill) on 5th May 1964.

J. R. P. Hunt

Plate 94 (below right): The crew of 0-6-0 No. 3217 take a rest from duties on an engineer's train, and give a glance at No. 7919 *Runter Hall* heading for Birmingham, past Rowington, with an empty stock working during the summer of 1963.

J. R. P. Hunt

Plate 92 (below left): 8th August 1956 was a hot summer's day, and 'Modified Hall' No. 7925 *Westol Hall* is seen with no exhaust, hauling the 'down' 'Cornishman' out of Par, as it starts the steep 6½ mile climb to Burngullow.

L. Elsey

The 5600 class 0-6-2Ts

At the Grouping, the Great Western inherited many 0-6-2Ts from the railways of South Wales. Many of these were in poor condition, which resulted in a motive power shortage. Collett decided to scrap those in bad order, and rebuild the others with standard Churchward boilers and other standard parts. He also decided to continue the 0-6-2T wheel arrangement, which had not been used by the Great Western to any extent in the past.

No. 5600 appeared in November 1924, and two hundred had been built by 1928, the last fifty being built by Armstrong Whitworth. The majority of the class worked in South Wales, particularly in the Cardiff area, but these locomotives could also be found around Wolverhampton, Bristol, Swindon and Westbury.

They were extremely versatile locomotives, with impressive power and acceleration. The first withdrawals were in 1962, and all had gone by 1966. Several have been preserved.

Plate 95 (left): No. 5675, recently ex-works, pictured on 3rd June 1963 and in unlined green livery, is seen on Swansea East Dock Depot.

Gavin Morrison

Plate 96 (below): One of the preserved 5600 class locomotives, No. 6697, is seen on 19th April 1956, leaving Leamington Spa Yard with an 'up' freight. This was one of the Armstrong Whitworth locomotives built in 1928. It appears to have a tall safety-valve bonnet, although these were not originally fitted to the Armstrong Whitworth locomotives.

R. C. Riley

Plate 97 (right): No. 6628 enters Quakers Yard (High Level), on 10th August 1963, with a train from Aberdare to Pontypool Road. The locomotive was one of the Swindon-built batch of 1927.

J. R. P. Hunt

Plate 98 (below): No. 5667, built in June 1926 and in lined British Railways Brunswick green livery, is seen on 3rd June 1962 on Barry Shed, together with three pannier tanks.

Gavin Morrison

Plate 99 (right): A train of empty coal wagons is pictured on 12th May 1952, passing Penrhos Junction, just west of Caerphilly, headed by No. 5653 in the plain black livery.

R. C. Riley

The 6000 class 4-6-0 'Kings'

Volumes have been written in praise of these magnificent machines, which were really the ultimate development over twenty years of Churchward's 'Stars'. Much speculation surrounds the reasons for the building of the 'Kings', but the Publicity Department, no doubt, had much to do with it.

The 20 ton axle load restriction imposed by the Civil Engineer had stifled further development of the 'Castles', but with the limit being raised for the Plymouth and Wolverhampton routes to 22½ tons upon instruction from the General Manager, the way was clear for the 'Kings'.

Tests with No. 5001 *Llandovery Castle* resulted in a reduction in the coupled wheels diameter to 6ft. 6in. Another departure from the standard design was the leading bogie, with outside bearings for the leading axle, and inside for the trailing; this was necessary to give adequate clearance on curves.

No. 6000 *King George V* appeared in June 1927 in time to be shipped to America for the Baltimore & Ohio Railroad Centenary.

The Great Western had the most powerful express locomotive in the country, without it being a Pacific, with little variation within the class of thirty. After some small adjustments to improve the riding qualities, the 'Kings' settled down to give splendid service on the jobs for which they were designed.

It was in 1947 that Hawksworth fitted No. 6022 with a four-row superheated boiler and a mechanical lubricator, with some improvement in performance. After tests with No. 6001 in 1953, No. 6015 appeared in September 1955 with a double chimney and double blastpipe. The performance of this locomotive was superb, resulting in the whole class receiving the modifications, plus new cylinders, new half frames, valve gear and motion parts. It was in this condition that the 'Kings' gave their finest performances.

Plate 100 (above): On 15th July 1937, a well-polished Wolverhampton (Stafford Road) 'King', No. 6006 *King George I*, prepares to leave Paddington at the head of the 7.10p.m. departure for Wolverhampton.

J. P. Wilson

Focus on No. 6000 *King George V*

Plate 101 (above): A close up of the bell, presented by the Baltimore & Ohio Railway to commemorate the visit of the locomotive to the centenary celebrations in 1927. Two cabside medallions were also presented. At this date, 23rd April 1962, the bell was mounted on a wooden plinth.

Gavin Morrison

Plate 102 (above): After working the 'down' 'Inter-City' from Paddington on 20th July 1954, No. 6000 *King George V* prepares to turn on the Wolverhampton (Stafford Road) turntable. The locomotive was ex-works in April 1954, and is seen with an inner sleeved chimney and modified outside steam pipes, and mechanical lubricator. During its 35 years of service, it covered 1,910,424 miles, being withdrawn in December 1962 for preservation at the Bulmer Railway Centre, Hereford.

B. Morrison

Plate 103 (below): The 'down' 'Cambrian Coast Express' pulls out of Paddington headed by No. 6000 *King George V* on 6th August 1960.

R. C. Riley

Plate 104 (above): In keeping with the trend of the mid-1930s, the Great Western decided to partially streamline No. 6014 *King Henry VII*, which totally ruined the classical looks of the locomotive. Fortunately, only 'Castle' class locomotive No. 5005 *Manorbier Castle* and *King Henry VII* received this treatment. No. 6014 emerged from Swindon Works in this condition in March 1935, but by January 1943 all signs of streamlining had gone, except the 'V' shaped cab. Of particular interest is the streamline fairing on the tender, which only lasted a matter of months.

British Rail/OPC Collection

Plate 105 (below): Restored to its former glory, but still with the 'V' shaped cab, and with its reporting number indicator fitted above the buffer beam, No. 6014 *King Henry VII* makes a splendid sight as it passes High Wycombe on 6th May 1957, heading the 2.10p.m. Paddington to Birkenhead express. The locomotive spent a great deal of its 34 years on this route. During its life, it covered 1,830,386 miles.

J. D. Edwards

Plate 106 (above): Very light work for No. 6002 *King William IV* as it prepares to leave Leamington Spa with an 'up' local train on 19th February 1949. The unique front bogie design shows up well in this picture.

J. P. Wilson

Plate 107 (right): No. 6016 *King Edward V* receives attention at Old Oak Common before setting off for Paddington to work a 'down' express in 1953.

Gavin Morrison

Plate 108 (below): Journey's end for an express from Birkenhead to Paddington, on 15th July 1937, headed by No. 6006 *King George I*, which spent most of its working life at Wolverhampton (Stafford Road) Depot. It was in fact the first 'King' to be withdrawn, in February 1962.

J. P. Wilson

'Kings' on the 'Cornish Riviera Express'

Plate 109 (left): No. 6004 *King George III* glistens in the winter sunshine on 1st December 1957, as it passes under the bridge at Old Oak Common at the head of the 'down' train. This was the first 'King' to receive a cast-iron double chimney.

R. C. Riley

Plate 110 (below): No. 6000 *King George V* with its bell and plaques beautifully turned out by Old Oak Common Shed, races out of Sonning Cutting with the regulator closed giving a pleasing smoke effect, on the 'down' train in 1953.

M. W. Earley

Plate 111 (above): No. 6022 *King George III*, the first 'King' to be fitted with a four-row superheater, in February 1948, is seen in Sonning Cutting, at the location made famous by the late Maurice Earley.

M. W. Earley

Plate 112 (below): With a train of this size, plenty of assistance will be needed over the South Devon banks for No. 6017 *King Edward IV*, seen skirting the River Teign, just west of Teignmouth, with a 'down' express on 22nd June 1958.

L. Elsey

Plate 113 (above): On 5th June 1949, No. 6018 *King Henry VI* makes a magnificent sight as it leaves Exeter St. David's with a Bristol to Plymouth express. This locomotive took part in the 'Locomotive Exchanges' in 1948, and ran between King's Cross and Leeds.

J. P. Wilson

Plate 114 (below): A sad day for 'King' enthusiasts was 28th April 1962, when, No. 6018 *King Henry VI* was reinstated after withdrawal to work the last 'King' trip from Birmingham, via Southall, to Swindon. One of the authors was a passenger on the train, and still vividly remembers the fantastic climb of Hatton Bank. The locomotive is pictured on Swindon Shed, surrounded by Hymek diesels.

Gavin Morrison

Plate 115 (above):   On 14th March 1957, the 'down' 'Inter-City' is seen departing High Wycombe, en route to Wolverhampton, headed by 'King' No. 6007 *King William III*. It was said to be virtually a new locomotive after rebuilding due to the Shrivenham collision of 15th January 1936.

J. D. Edwards

Plate 116 (below):   'King' No. 6001 *King Edward VII* approaches High Wycombe with the up 7.25 Wolverhampton to Paddington train on 21st March 1957.   *J. D. Edwards*

Plate 117 (below):   The 'down' 'Inter-City' express, without headboard, bursts out of White House Farm Tunnel headed by 'King' No. 6028 *King George VI* on 18th March 1957.

J. D. Edwards

Plate 118 (left): The final form fo
No. 6000 *King George V*, seen or
Westbury Shed on 23rd April 1962.
Gavin Morrison

Plate 119 (above): On 5th June 1938, No. 6029 *King Edward VIII* is pictured on Bristol (Bath Road) Shed sporting the locomotive's pre-war livery. No. 6029 was named *King Stephen* until May 1936.

J. P. Wilson

Plate 120 (below): The end of the road for Nos. 6003 *King George IV* and 6024 *King Edward I*, seen stored at Cardiff (Canton) Depot on 3rd June 1962; both had done their last working and were withdrawn in that month. No. 6024 is preserved and is currently being restored.

Gavin Morrison

The 5700 class 0-6-0 Pannier Tanks

By 1929, there was a growing need to replace the hundreds of aged saddle and pannier tanks, which operated throughout the Great Western system.

No. 5700 appeared from the North British Locomotive Company works in 1929, and became the first of no fewer than 863 locomotives.

Seven different builders were used in the construction of these locomotives, spanning a period of 21 years. There were minor differences between certain batches but, externally, the most obvious was the improved cab and top feed to the boiler; these modifications commencing with locomotive No. 8750 in 1933. There were ten locomotives built with condensing apparatus for use on the Metropolitan line.

Thirteen of the locomotives were sold to the London Transport Executive; three remaining in service until 1971. The first withdrawals were in 1956, but some survived until 1966. Due to regional boundary alterations, a few were allocated to the London Midland Region, whilst some others finished on the Southern working empty carriage stock workings out of Waterloo, and on the Folkestone Harbour branch.

They were extremely successful machines, very powerful for their size, free running, and with excellent acceleration.

Plate 121 (right): This pleasing picture, taken in July 1959, is made interesting by the human element, and shows No. 8762, still with GWR lettering, carrying out shunting duties at Westbourne Park, London. *J. B. Snell*

Plate 122 (below): This excellent branch line scene shows No. 9647 at Chard (Central), on 27th June 1958, working a Taunton to Chard Junction train. This locomotive was built in 1946 at Swindon.

J. P. Wilson

Plate 123 (above): One of the 25 pannier tanks built by W. G. Bagnall in 1930 and 1931 was No. 8744, pictured at Westbury Shed on 1st October 1961.

Gavin Morrison

Plate 124 (above): Another W. G. Bagnall example is No. 6707, pictured at Swindon Works on 7th June 1959. The fifty locomotives in the 6700 series were only fitted with steam brakes and a simple three link coupling for shunting work. Many of the first batch of twenty five were stored, when new, for two years as there was no work for them. Most of this batch of locomotives spent their working life in South Wales.

Gavin Morrison

Plate 125 (right): No. 9707 was one of the ten locomotives built with condensing apparatus for use on the Metropolitan line, which were always based at Old Oak Common Shed. They had a slightly increased water tank capacity, but a reduced coal capacity. The batch were fitted with ATC apparatus, which was raised when running on electrified track.

B. Morrison

Plate 126 (below): Spark arresting chimneys were fitted to thirteen of the pannier tanks. Nos. 5757 and 7713 had them fitted in 1937 and 1938, but the rest were altered during World War II. The locomotives used in military depots around Didcot were the ones to be modified. No. 5744 is pictured stored at Didcot with other pannier tanks in September 1959.

Gavin Morrison

Panniers at Work

Plate 127 (above): One of the locomotives built in 1930 by Armstrong Whitworth, No. 7788, is seen in 1945 in Sonning Cutting heading a pick-up freight to Reading (West) Junction Yard. The fireman looks anxiously to see if the injector is working.

M. W. Earley

Plate 128 (right): Someone appears to be about to leave the footplate on this picture of No. 4643, as it arrives at Park Junction with a train of pit props from Newport Docks on 11th March 1959.

S. Rickard

Plate 129 (below): On 16th May 1959, No. 7736, a North British-built pannier tank of 1929, pauses at Torpantau with a passenger train from Brecon to Newport, after completing the steep climb from Talyllyn Junction on the old Brecon & Merthyr line.

S. Rickard

The 2251 class 0-6-0s

The Churchward 2-6-0s and 2-8-0s had taken over main line freight duties, which left a shortage of small freight/mixed traffic locomotives for the lines on which the larger locomotives were prohibited. Collett produced 120 locomotives of the 2251 class, which were really a tender version of the 5700 panniers. They replaced many of the famous 'Dean Goods' engines, and were well liked by the crews. No. 2251 appeared in 1930, whilst the last, No. 3219, emerged in 1948.

Plate 130 (above): No. 3212, with a Churchward 3,000 gallon tender, was built in 1947 and is seen at the back of Westbury Shed on 1st October 1961.

Gavin Morrison

Plate 131 (right): An 'up' pick-up freight from Banbury, on 4th March 1957, approaches the outskirts of High Wycombe, headed by No. 2297.

J. D. Edwards

Plate 132 (left): On 21st June 1959, No. 2247, built just at the end of World War II, is seen at Worcester Shed. Numbers 2281-2286 were built new with tenders from the 'Aberdares', which were of 4,000 gallon capacity, and originally came from the Robinson 2-8-0 RODs. Ten other members of the class were fitted with these tenders from time to time.

Gavin Morrison

Plate 133 (right): Collett 0-6-0 No. 2297 heads the 9.40a.m. Acton to Banbury pick-up away from High Wycombe on 15th April 1957.

J. D. Edwards

Plate 134 (below): On 10th September 1962, No. 3201 poses at Talyllyn Junction Station, in fully lined out passenger green livery. It is waiting for a connection off the Mid-Wales line, before heading up the valley to Torpantau, at the head of a Brecon to Newport local train.

Gavin Morrison

Plate 135 (left): On 30th March 1959, eleven years after nationalisation, No. 7428 still has GWR lettering on the tank sides. It is seen at Blaenau Ffestiniog (Central) ready to leave on a single coach train for Bala Junction. Fifty of the 7400 class locomotives were built between 1936 and 1950, and they had an increased boiler pressure of 180lb., compared to the 165lb. of the 6400 locomotives, which made them slightly more powerful.

Gavin Morrison

Plate 136 (below): In lined green BR livery, No 6416 prepares to leave Merthyr on 10th September 1962. All forty locomotives of the 6400 class were fitted for auto-train working, and were primarily used in the steeply-graded lines of the South Wales valleys. They were built between 1932 and 1937, and three examples have been preserved.

Gavin Morrison

Plate 137 (right): On 29th March 1959, No. 7428 comes off the train from Blaenau Ffestiniog (Central) at Bala, and heads for the shed. No. 8727 waits to take over for the short journey to Bala Junction, to connect with trains on the Ruabon to Barmouth line.

Gavin Morrison

Plate 138 (left): The 5400 class locomotives were designed for passenger work, particularly auto-train working. They had 5ft. 2in. coupled wheels, which were larger than the 5700 class (4ft. 7½in.) and were Collett's answer as a replacement for the aged 0-6-0 pannier tanks which had been auto-fitted late in life. They were fast with excellent acceleration, and could normally be seen sandwiched between four auto-trailers. No. 5410 is pictured on 25th February 1962, in fully lined out BR green livery, at Westbury, but out of use. Withdrawals started as early as 1956 with the demise of the branch lines, and the introduction of diesel multiple units.

Gavin Morrison

Plate 139 (right): No. 5418 operates push and pull duties in May 1952, on the West Ealing to Greenford line.

C. R. L. Coles

The 4800, 1400 and 5800 class 0-4-2Ts

These splendid little 0-4-2Ts were another of Collett's master-pieces. Ninety five were built during five years in the mid-1930s, and they could be seen at work over most of the Great Western system. There was some similarity with the Armstrong 517 class, but the locomotives were built with standard components used on the 5400 and 6400 classes. The 4800 locomotives, which later became the 1400s, were fitted for auto-working and with ATC, whilst the 5800 series had neither. Nos. 4800 to 4874 were re-numbered due to the 481 numbers being required for oil burning 2800s. The final members of the class lasted until 1964, and many have been preserved.

Plate 140 (above left): On 16th June 1957, No. 1438 stands on Stourbridge Junction Shed during a visit by a group of enthusiasts from the north of England.

Gavin Morrison

Plate 141 (left): One of the non auto-fitted batch of twenty built in 1933 is seen at Bristol (Temple Meads) on 4th June 1949, with a High Siphon van, used for milk churn traffic.

J. P. Wilson

Plate 142 (below): Still sporting the Great Western livery, in August 1952, No. 1432 leaves Oswestry with the 11.20 train to Gobowen. This was an auto-train working for many years.

B. Morrison

Plate 143 (right): Fully lined out, in November 1953, No. 1411 prepares to leave Aylesbury Town with the 1.25p.m. train to Princes Risborough. Prior to 1953, these workings were shared with Eastern Region locomotives and stock. The locomotive has a top feed added to the boiler, and a large whistle shield to stop steam obscuring the cab windows.

N. W. Sprinks

Plate 144 (below): One of the Collett 0-4-2T locomotives fitted for auto-working is seen at Wallingford ready to leave for Cholsey & Moulsford on the main line. By 6th March 1959, the locomotive shed at Wallingford had closed. The capacity of the water tower should be more than adequate to fill the tanks of No. 1407.

J. D. Edwards

Plate 145 (left): A delightful setting for this photograph of No. 1437 and auto-car No. W1670W, recovering from a signal check at Princes Risborough, with the 2.42p.m. ex-Oxford on 1st April 1957. Both tracks are single lines, the one on the left being the Watlington branch.

J. D. Edwards

Plate 146 (below): The Hemyock branch was the home of a 1400 class engine for many years. It left the main line at Tiverton Junction with two delightful intermediate halts at Uffculme and Culmstock. On 8th October 1962, No. 1451 is pictured at Hemyock looking very smart in its fully lined out BR Brunswick green livery.

L. Elsey

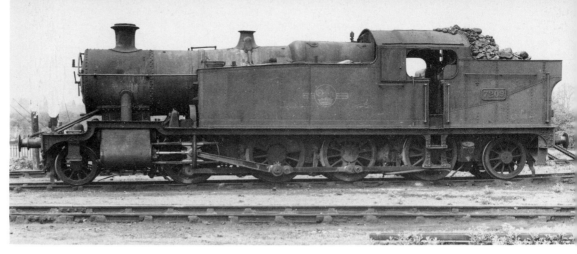

Plate 147 (right): No. 7209 is pictured at Severn Tunnel Junction Shed on 26th April 1964. This locomotive was rebuilt from 2-8-0T No. 5284 in October 1934 and the first batch of twenty, Nos. 7200 to 7219, retained the curved platform above the cylinders.

Gavin Morrison

The 7200 class 2-8-2Ts

There were 54 of these fine machines rebuilt from the 4200 and 5205 class 2-8-0Ts, between August 1934 and December 1939. The frames on the first forty were increased in length by 4ft. 1in. at the rear to accommodate the trailing radial axle. Seven hundred additional gallons of water could be carried, with three tons more coal, which considerably extended the area of operation of the class. The first forty were rebuilt from the 5205 class, whilst the last fourteen were from the much older 4200 class. In fact, No. 4202, which became No. 7242, was 25 years old at rebuilding. They were extremely good machines, most being based in South Wales, and, in their early years, regularly worked trains to London and Exeter. No. 7235 was tried on the Lickey Incline, but had problems with platform clearance at Bromsgrove. The water capacity on the last fourteen members was 900 extra gallons, but only two tons extra coal.

Plate 148 (above right): Light work for Oxford-based 7200 class locomotive No. 7239, rebuilt from 5205 class No. 5274, heading for home at Kingham on 2nd March 1960.

J. D. Edwards

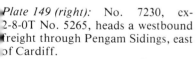

Plate 149 (right): No. 7230, ex-2-8-0T No. 5265, heads a westbound freight through Pengam Sidings, east of Cardiff.

S. Rickard

Plate 150 (above): No. 7216, which was originally 2-8-0T No. 5291, passes through Llantrisant with a heavy eastbound coal train on 14th August 1963.

J. R. P. Hunt

Plate 151 (below): The immaculate external condition of No. 7215, after a visit to the works, is unlikely to last long after a few weeks work around the South Wales coalfield. It is pictured at Swansea East Dock on 9th September 1962.

Gavin Morrison

The 1366 class 0-6-0 Pannier Tanks

Only six of these delightful little tanks were built by Collett, in 1934, and were basically an improved version of the 1361 class, introduced by Churchward. They were used initially within Swindon Works, and later at Weymouth Docks as seen in these pictures. Finally they went to the Southern Region's Wenford Bridge mineral branch where they replaced the famous Beattie 2-4-0 well tanks. No. 1369 is preserved.

Plates 153 to 156: A series of pictures taken on 30th September 1961, at Weymouth Docks, of locomotives Nos. 1368 and 1369, handling two Channel Island boat trains. Clearance was extremely limited along the quayside, and railway staff had to frequently 'bounce' cars out of the way. They were fitted with bells to warn unwary pedestrians as, presumably, it was thought that a sharp blast on the whistle would frighten people too much.

Gavin Morrison

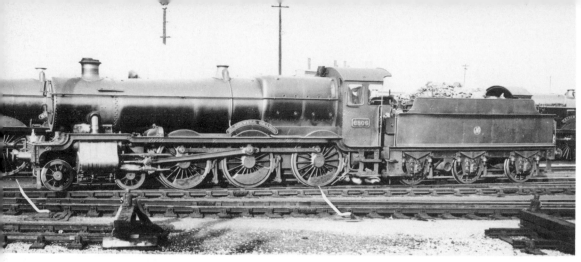

Plate 157 (left): No. 6806 *Blackwell Grange* stands on Bristol (Bath Road) Shed in its original livery, on 5th March 1938, with a 3,500 gallon Churchward tender, and with a short copper-capped chimney. Note the fire iron casing along the bottom of the firebox.

J. P. Wilson

The 6800 class 4-6-0 'Granges'

The 'Granges' were the result of the withdrawal of eighty 4300 class Moguls, although in fact only the wheels and motion were used. The locomotives had the same route availability as the 'Halls', and so were, in fact, more restricted than the Moguls. The coupled wheel diameter was 5ft. 8in., which was slightly smaller than the 'Halls'. The first four engines were initially fitted with a plain cast-iron chimney. The locomotives were used throughout the GWR system, on similar duties to the 'Halls'.

Plate 158 (below): Fresh from overhaul at Swindon Works in June 1959 is No. 6811 *Cranbourne Grange* in fully lined out Brunswick green livery, and still attached to one of the small 3,500 gallon tenders. The locomotive is fitted with a narrow chimney.

Gavin Morrison

Plate 159 (right): On 16th July 1964, No. 6871 *Bourton Grange* takes the centre road at Leamington Station at the head of a coke train. The locomotive is obviously recently ex-works and has the 4,000 gallon tender attached. It also carries a Midland Region shed-plate (2B).

J. R. P. Hunt

Plate 160 (below): A superb study of No. 6842 *Nunhold Grange* making a spirited ascent of Hatton Bank with a 'down' express on 27th September 1964.

J. R. P. Hunt

Plate 161 (left): Worcester-allocated No. 6851 *Hurst Grange* is seen re starting a 'down' express for Cheste at Shrewsbury on 9th August 1956.

B. Morrison

Plate 162 (below): An extremely dirty member of the class, No. 6868 *Penrhos Grange*, is seen at Eastleigh Station on 12th September 1964, as i pauses with a rake of Southern stock on a York to Bournemouth express Great Western locomotives used to work through to Bournemouth, nor mally being attached to the trains a Banbury or Oxford.

Gavin Morrison

Plate 163 (right): An extraordinary working occurred on 15th August 1964, when No. 6858 *Woolston Grange*, working the Poole to Bradford /Leeds train, and which would normally have come off at Leicester or Nottingham, managed, due to an oversight by control, to reach Huddersfield. As can be seen from the cylinder casing, it hit the platform edge at Berry Brow, between Penistone and Huddersfield. The photographer was able to grab a quick picture of it on Hillhouse Shed, Huddersfield, before an astonished foreman ejected him from the premises and placed the locomotive well out of sight inside the shed, where it remained for two weeks before being towed to Crewe as an out of gauge load.

Gavin Morrison

Plate 164 (centre): No. 6831 *Bearley Grange* is pictured on 23rd July 1961, in Swindon Works yard with the preserved 'Dean Goods' and *Lode Star*, and fitted with a 4,000 gallon tender in fully lined out green livery.

W. Potter, D. Cobbe Collection

Plate 165 (bottom): No. 6831, as it ended its career, dumped without name and number plates, and with a 3,500 gallon tender at Oxley Depot some four years later, in October 1965.

Gavin Morrison

The 7800 class 4-6-0 'Manors'

The first of the class appeared in January 1938, twenty locomotives being built in the initial batch. Like the 'Granges', the first batch of 'Manors' utilised the wheels and motion from withdrawn 4300 class Moguls. It is ironic that these locomotives were the last built by Collett and, in their original form, were the least successful. A new standard boiler No. 24 was used and this proved to be a poor steam producer, and it was not until 1951 that tests with improved draughting were carried out with No. 7818 *Granville Manor* that the problems were solved. The locomotives were attached to 3,500 gallon Churchward tenders, although some acquired the 'intermediate' 3,500 gallon type. The 17 ton axle loading gave them an extensive route availability, which is no doubt why so many have been preserved. The class ultimately received fully lined Brunswick green livery from British Railways.

Plate 166 (left): No. 7814 *Fringford Manor*, built in January 1939, and recently ex-Swindon Works when this picture was taken on 8th September 1962, at Derry Ormond on the Carmarthen to Aberystwyth line.

Gavin Morrison

Plate 167 (below): No. 7802 *Bradley Manor* on 'special' duties for the Stephenson Locomotive Society at Oswestry Station, when it headed the last train over the Whitchurch to Oswestry section of the ex-Cambrian Railways, on 17th January 1965.

Gavin Morrison

Plate 168 (right): For many years, especially during the 1950s and early 1960s, Aberystwyth Depot always seemed to make a special effort to keep an immaculate 'Manor' available for working the 'Cambrian Coast Express' to Shrewsbury. No. 7803 *Barcote Manor* was frequently chosen for this special attention along with Nos. 7802 and 7819. It is seen on shed at Aberystwyth with a London Midland Region (6F) shed-plate, and fitted with an 'intermediate' 3,500 gallon tender.

J. Livesey

Plate 169 (left): The 'down' 'Cambrian Coast Express' split at Dovey Junction releasing carriages for Pwllheli. The Aberystwyth section went forward behind the locomotive which had brought the train from Shrewsbury. The three coach train was easy work for No. 7803 *Barcote Manor*, on 30th May 1964, as it drifts into Borth Station.

Gavin Morrison

Plate 170 (below): After working the 'down' 'Cambrian Coast Express' on 30th May 1964, No. 7803 *Barcote Manor* simmers gently on Aberystwyth Shed.

Gavin Morrison

Plate 174 (above): Another of the well-kept Aberystwyth 'Manors', No. 7819 *Hinton Manor*, prepares to leave Shrewsbury with the 'down' 'Cambrian Coast Express' on 31st March 1964.

J. Livesey

Plate 173 (above): On a very warm day in May 1964, a very dirty No. 7800 *Torquay Manor* approaches Talerdigg Summit, on the Cambrian main line, with a Gainsborough Model Railway Society's special, en route to Aberystwyth to visit the Vale of Rheidol narrow gauge railway.

Gavin Morrison

Plate 175 (below): A portrait of No. 7812 *Erlestoke Manor*, which is now preserved on the Severn Valley Railway. The photograph was taken on 8th September 1962, outside Aberystwyth Station.

Gavin Morrison

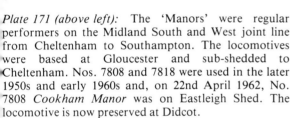

Plate 171 (above left): The 'Manors' were regular performers on the Midland South and West joint line from Cheltenham to Southampton. The locomotives were based at Gloucester and sub-shedded to Cheltenham. Nos. 7808 and 7818 were used in the later 1950s and early 1960s and, on 22nd April 1962, No. 7808 *Cookham Manor* was on Eastleigh Shed. The locomotive is now preserved at Didcot.

Gavin Morrison

Plate 176 (right): Waiting to depart from Aberystwyth with an express for Manchester on 8th September 1962, is No. 7822 *Foxcote Manor*, which was one of the batch of ten built as late as December 1950.

Gavin Morrison

Plate 172 (left): An unusual setting for this picture of No. 7809 *Childrey Manor* as it passes Wye Valley Junction on 18th October 1958, en route to South Wales with a 'down' vans train.

S. Rickard

The Hawksworth Era

The 1000 class 4-6-0 'Counties'

F. W. Hawksworth was Chief Mechanical Engineer from July 1941 to 1946, and he is probably best known for the 'County' class. The 'County' design, when it appeared in August 1945, was not so different from Great Western traditions as had been rumoured. The main new features were the double blast-pipe and chimney, a non standard coupled wheel diameter of 6ft. 3in., and a high boiler pressure of 280lb. The power from the two cylinders was roughly equivalent to the four cylinders of a 'Castle', this causing considerable increase in hammer blow, which together with the weight of the coupled wheels of 19 tons 14 cwt. per axle, resulted in the class having speed restrictions on all routes other than where the 'Kings' were permitted. In the early days, all tended to be allocated to sheds covering the Paddington to Penzance, and Paddington to Wolverhampon routes. These restrictions were lifted to some degree, resulting in the class having a wider sphere of operation. The reason for the construction of the class in the first place is not entirely clear, as the work they carried out was generally inferior to the 'Castles', and it is significant that only thirty were built. The first locomotive, No. 1000, was the first to emerge from Swindon in Great Western green livery after World War II.

Plate 177 (above): The distinctive nameplate attached to No. 1000, after running without one for approximately one year.
B. Morrison

Plate 178 (below): No. 1000 *County of Middlesex* is seen in British Railways lined black livery, ready to leave Paddington with a 'down' express on 8th July 1952. This locomotive was the only one to be constructed with a copper-capped double chimney and, in this state, was a poor performer. After tests and alteration to draughting in 1954, the rest of the class, which had single chimneys, were altered to squat copper-capped chimneys, which ruined the appearance but improved the performance.
J. P. Wilson

Plate 179 (above): On a lovely summer's evening in August 1958, No. 1025 *County of Radnor* drifts into Stratford-upon-Avon with empty stock, which was to form a returning excursion to Manchester (London Road).

B. Morrison

Plate 180 (below): A superb portrait of No. 1015 *County of Gloucester*, straight out of Swindon Works after overhaul, and painted in British Railways lined black livery. It is seen in Reading Shed yard in 1949 and it appears that the works have forgotten to fix the front numberplate, hence the chalked number on the buffer beam. This locomotive ran for thirteen months before being named.

M. W. Earley

Plate 181 (above): Plymouth (Laira)-based No. 1010 *County of Caernarvon*, resplendent in British Railways Brunswick green livery, on 26th June 1955, outside Swindon Works, after a general overhaul, and ready for running in, before returning south to do battle with the South Devon banks.

W. Potter, D. Cobbe Collection

Plate 182 (below): Plenty of help seems to be at hand to push the coal forward on Shrewsbury-based No. 1017 *County of Hereford* as it pauses at Bristol (Temple Meads) whilst working the 'down' 14.55 Paignton – Wolverhampton express on 7th July 1956.

J. P. Wilson

Plate 183 (right): An interesting comparison with *Plate 175* of the second double chimney fitted to the first Hawksworth 'County', No. 1000 *County of Middlesex*, as it passes East Main box at Reading in March 1960, at the head of the 1.45a.m. 'up' express from Bristol (Temple Meads) to Paddington. The 82A shed plate indicated that the locomotive was allocated to Bristol (Bath Road) Depot at this time.

M. W. Earley

Plate 184 (below): A powerful picture of No. 1028 *County of Warwick* nearing the summit of Hatton Bank with a 'down' freight in 1963.

J. R. P. Hunt

Plate 185 (top left): The midsummer weather has ruined any chance of some exhaust from No. 1018 *County of Leicester*, as it pulls away round the sharp curve from Shrewsbury Station with the 'up' 11.40a.m. Birkenhead to Paddington express on 23rd June 1962.

John Whiteley

Plate 186 (above): The end of the line for No. 1014 *County of Glamorgan* as it awaits its fate at the back of Swindon on 26th April 1964, after 18 years of service. Note the wooden numberplate which had been attached; it is not known if the nameplate was genuine.

Gavin Morrison

Plate 187 (centre): The ugly short double chimney shows up clearly in this portrait of No. 1013 *County of Dorset* at its home depot of Swindon on 26th April 1964. It was one of the very few members of the class still in active service by this date.

Gavin Morrison

Plate 188 (left): By 20th September 1964, No. 1011 *County of Chester* was the only active member of the class, and on this date it ran a farewell tour from Birmingham to Swindon Works, where it is seen in this photograph. The nameplate is in fact a replacement which was hurriedly made for the occasion, as the original was stolen only a few days before the tour. The locomotive was originally allocated the name *County of Cheshire*, but as this was already carried by one of the 3800 class, it was altered to *County of Chester*.

J. R. P. Hunt

The 9400 class 0-6-0 Pannier Tanks

Further to a request for more 5700 class pannier tanks in 1947, the General Manager, Sir James Milne, insisted that a more modern-looking locomotive should be produced, and so Hawksworth designed the 9400 class, with the No. 10 taper boiler. The locomotives were not so easy to operate whilst shunting, as the controls were not as accessible as in the 5700 panniers. They were also heavier than the 5700 class pannier tanks, and had to be restricted over some routes, but in spite of their disadvantages British Railways built a total of 210, the last ones appearing as late as 1956, which gave them very short lives indeed. Only the first ten were built at Swindon under the Great Western in 1947, the rest being constructed by R. Stephenson, Bagnall & Co., and the Yorkshire Engine Company. Many were withdrawn with less than ten years of service and some must have been in good mechanical order, so it is rather surprising that only two members of the class have been preserved.

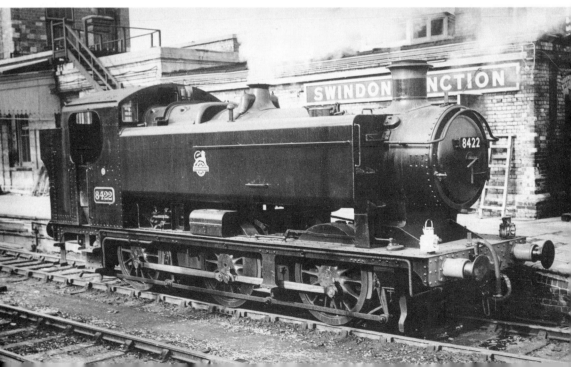

Plate 189 (above): Swindon-built No. 9401 is seen leaving Stratford-upon-Avon with a stopping train to Worcester on 14th December 1957. This locomotive was loaned to the Eastern Region for trials in 1957, and was used at Temple Mills Yards, London.

R. C. Riley

Plate 190 (right): One of the Bagnall-built locomotives, No. 8422, is pictured on shunting duties at Swindon Junction Station on 15th October 1950. Fifty engines were constructed by this company between 1949 and 1954.

L. Elsey

The 1500 class 0-6-0 Pannier Tanks

Only ten of these heavy duty shunting pannier tanks were produced in 1949 at Swindon. Hawksworth departed from the normal Great Western tradition for panniers, in that the 1500 class was designed with outside cylinders and Walschaerts valve gear. The short wheelbase of 12ft. 10in. allowed them to negotiate very sharp curves, but precluded them from being used at speed on the main line, as they became unsteady. They will be be remembered for their duties in dealing with empty carriage stock at Paddington. Some members of the class were sold to the National Coal Board after withdrawal from British Railways, and No. 1501 was rescued for preservation from this source.

Plate 191 (below): One of the three members of the class to receive the lined British Railways black livery was No. 1503. It is seen on 3rd October 1959, carrying out empty carriage stock duties at Westbourne Park, near Paddington.

R. C. Riley

The 1600 class 0-6-0 Pannier Tanks

This was another class of locomotive which was built too late by British Railways to have a useful working life. No. 1600 did not appear until 1949, and was the final design by Hawksworth. In spite of their late construction, seventy members of the class had been built by 1955. They were designed to be able to work all the lines, especially mineral branches, where the larger panniers were prohibited

Plate 192 (left): No. 1669, the last of the class to be built, in May 1955, was the last Great Western-designed locomotive to be built at Swindon, thus bringing to an end many Swindon traditions. After this date only BR Standard designs were constructed. It is pictured on 9th September 1962 at Whitland.

Gavin Morrison

The Absorbed Companies

The Barry Railway

Plate 193 (below): The Barry Railway Company came into existence in 1884, and started operation in 1888. The prime traffic, as with nearly all South Wales lines, was coal, and in 1913 it carried no less than eleven million tons. There were 65 route miles and 148 locomotives which were absorbed into the GWR in 1922. Most were 0-6-2 tank locomotives, but there were ten 0-6-4Ts, seven 0-8-2Ts and four 0-8-0s, which were definitely non standard for the GWR. In this scene, photographed on 5th June 1938, a Hosgood Class B1 0-6-2T, built by Sharp, Stewart & Co., in the 1890s, stands at Radyr Junction.

J. G. Dewing

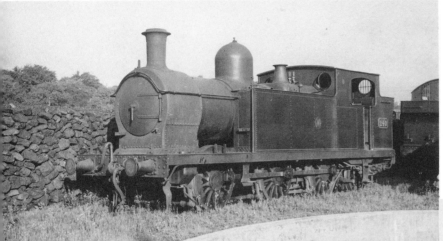

The Cambrian Railways

Plate 194 (below): A separate section is devoted to the Cambrian Railways Company in *Plates 214 to 229*. One of the 107 locomotives taken over by the GWR in 1922 was 0-6-0 No. 880. The class was built between 1894 and 1899, the locomotives being supplied by Neilson & Co., and Vulcan Foundry. No. 880 is pictured at Oswestry Depot on 14th September 1937.

J. G Dewing

The Alexandra (Newport & South Wales) Docks Railway

Plate 195 (below): The company was founded in 1865. A wide variety of locomotives, 39 in all, were absorbed by the GWR, one of which was this one, No. 680, which survived until 1948, outliving its sister engine by 22 years. It is seen on 14th September 1937 at Oswestry Shed.

J. G. Dewing

Plate 196 (below): Another class to last well into nationalisation from the Alexandra (Newport & South Wales) Docks Railway was the Hawthorn Leslie-built 2-6-2T. Only two locomotives were constructed in 1920, and No. 1205 is seen here at Cardiff (Canton) Shed on 23rd July 1955. It appears to be out of use and was in fact officially withdrawn the following year.

F. J. Bullock

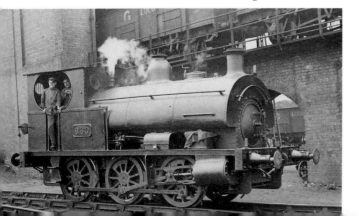

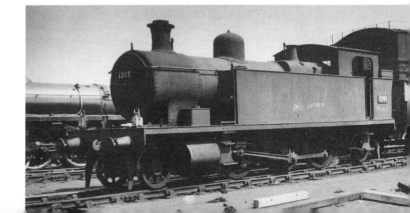

Plates 197 & 198: This was originally the Bute Docks Railway Company, which started as early as 1839 and was owned by the Second Marquis of Bute. It changed its name in 1897 to the Cardiff Railway Company. The GWR took over 36 locomotives in 1922. Most locomotives were either 0-6-0Ts or 0-6-2Ts, one of which was No. 681, an 0-6-0T, built in 1920 by Hudswell Clarke, which is pictured at Swindon on 24th April 1955. The railway also owned two Kitson-built 0-4-0 saddle tanks, Nos. 1338 and 1339. Constructed in 1898, No. 1338, shown here, is at Swansea East Dock on 9th September 1962, and lasted until 1963 when it was bought for preservation.

B. Morrison and Gavin Morrison

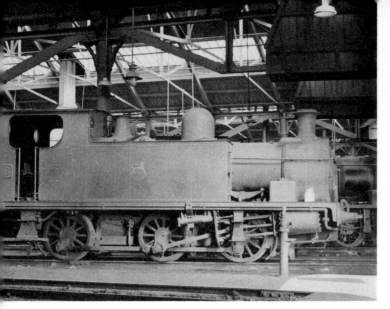

Plate 199 (above): No. 2198 was built in 1910 by Hudswell Clarke, and was in fact the only member of the class, although it was very similar to another 0-6-0T, built by the same company in 1909. Surprisingly, it lasted until 1959, and it is seen on 13th May 1956, inside Llanelly Shed.

B. Morrison

Plate 200 (above): No. 2176 was an Avonside saddle tank, constructed in 1907, and again was the only member of the class. It was originally named *Pembrey* but the nameplate was removed in 1927. In this picture it is out of use at Swindon Works dump, on 24th April 1955.

B. Morrison

The Burry Port & Gwendraeth Valley Railway

Plate 201 (right): The BP&GVR was only a small company which passed over fifteen locomotives to the GWR, all of which were 0-6-0Ts. The railway originated in 1865, being a development of a canal, harbour and tramway system, dating back as far as 1765. It was not until 1909 that the line handled any passenger traffic. Locomotive No. 2194, built by Avonside in 1903, is seen during her spell of duty with sister locomotive No. 2195 at Weymouth Docks, shunting coaches on 1st July 1935, a very wet day.

J. G. Dewing

Plate 202 (right): On 21st June 1955, lying outside Swindon Works cutting-up shop, is Hudswell Clarke 0-6-0T No. 2166. The class was built between 1909 and 1919. Seven of these locomotives were built, the first being withdrawn in 1929 and the last in 1956.

B. Morrison

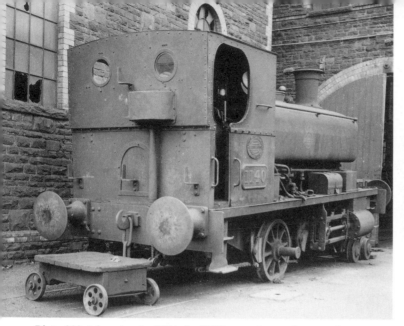

Plate 203 (above): In 1854 the SHT came into existence. It was a small company which handed over to the GWR eleven 0-4-0 saddle tanks and three 0-6-0 saddle tanks. No. 701, which became No. 1140 after 1948, was an Andrew Barclay locomotive, constructed in 1905. It is under repair on 21st July 1957 at Danygraig Depot.

B. Morrison

Plate 204 (above): No. 1145, originally No. 1098 until 1950, was a small 0-4-0 saddle tank built by Peckett in 1918, which survived until 1960. The locomotive is at Danygraig Depot on 21st July 1957.

B. Morrison

Plate 205 (below): A delightful study of No. 1142, originally No. 943, shunting at Clee Hill Summit in Shropshire on 15th August 1958. This locomotive was the only member of the class built in 1911 by Hudswell Clarke and lasted until 1959.

B. Morrison

The Swansea Harbour Trust

The Rhymney Railway

Plate 206 (left): Locomotives designed by Harry Riches formed the backbone of this railway's stock. The company's network basically comprised 51 miles of track, and the company started in 1858. One hundred and twenty three locomotives were taken over by the GWR and No. 65, rebuilt with a Swindon taper boiler, was built in 1909 being an A class by Harry Riches. It is heading west through Cardiff (General) with a freight on 2nd October 1953. Twenty four of these locomotives were built, lasting until 1955.

S. Rickard

Plate 208 (below): A view of Cardiff East Dock Depot on 12th May 1957, showing R class 0-6-2T No. 36 in company with more modern GWR tanks.

J. D. Edwards

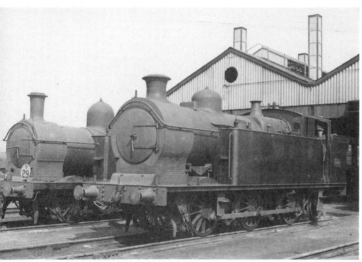

Plate 207 (above): Harry Riches R class locomotive, No 44, without its Swindon taper boiler, is seen at Radyr Junction Depot on 21st July 1938.

J. G. Dewing

Plate 209 (below): Another view of No. 36, as seen in *Plate 208*, at Cardiff East Docks.

J. D. Edwards

Plate 210 (below): No. 41 heads a Cardiff East Docks to Llanbradach Colliery freight through Heath Junction, on the former Rhymney main line, on 12th February 1953.

S. Rickard

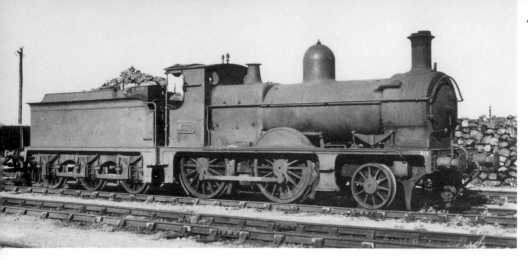

The Midland & South Western Junction Railway

Plate 211 (left): The MSWJR was formed in 1884 from two other companies, but it was not until 1891 that the line operated throughout from Andoversford Junction, near Cheltenham, to Red Posts Junction, just outside Andover. Twenty nine locomotives were absorbed in 1923, consisting of eight classes, including 4-4-4Ts. The locomotives were kept immaculate by the MSWJR, but No. 1334, which is one of three Dubs-built 2-4-0s of 1894, looks in a sorry state on 1st October 1954 at Didcot Depot.

J. G. Dewing

Powlesland & Mason

Plate 212 (right): P&M was not really a railway company, but a business owned by two gentlemen, which had its own locomotives for use on the Swansea Harbour Trust lines. The concern was started in 1865 and handed over nine locomotives in 1923 to the GWR. All were 0-4-0 saddle tanks, one of which was No. 779, renumbered in 1949 by the GWR to 1151. This was a Peckett, the class being built between 1912 and 1916, which survived until 1963. It is seen on Danygraig Depot, Swansea in 1957.

J. D. Edwards

The Taff Vale Railway

Plate 213 (left): By far the biggest, in terms of number of locomotives of the absorbed lines was the TVR. All 275 locomotives handed over were tank engines, mainly 0-6-2Ts. The first Taff Vale line from Cardiff to Merthyr opened in 1840. No. 373, seen awaiting scrap at Swindon on 8th September 1957, was a reboilered Cameron A class locomotive, built between 1914 and 1921.

Gavin Morrison

The Cambrian Lines

Plate 214 (below): The Cambrian Railways were the result of five companies joining together in 1904. This is possibly the most interesting and biggest in terms of mileage (300) of the absorbed companies. The system operated through the superb scenery of Mid-Wales, with its headquarters and workshops at Oswestry. Included in the 107 locomotives handed over in 1922 were the three narrow gauge engines of the Vale of Rheidol Railway, and the two of the Welshpool & Llanfair Railway, but the GWR immediately condemned 23 engines which reduced the figure to 84. The majority of the classes were 0-6-0 and 4-4-0 locomotives. No. 898, pictured at Oswestry on 7th April 1936, is an 0-6-0, the class being built by Sharp, Stewart between 1861 and 1873.

J. G. Dewing

Plate 215 (below): No. 895 is one of the large Belpaire-boilered goods locomotives known as the 15 class, which were very similar to the GWR 'Dean Goods' engines. These locomotives were built between 1903 and 1915 by Beyer Peacock and R. Stephenson. This view, photographed on 22nd July 1954, is at Oswestry Station, showing the 1.25p.m. arrival from Gobowen. The locomotive was withdrawn later in the year and was the last of the class.

B. Morrison

Plates 216 & 217: These delightful scenes, photographed on 18th July 1938, show the beautiful scenery through which the Cambrian main line passes. *Above* is a 4-4-0 'Dukedog', No. 3204 (later No. 9004 and formerly named *Earl of Dartmouth*), working a freight near Pontdolgoch. These locomotives were an ingenious rebuild by C. B. Collett, by taking a 'Bulldog' frame and mounting a 'Duke' class boiler. They lasted for more than twenty years on the ex-Cambrian lines. In the lower view 0-6-0 No. 896 climbs past Commins Coch with a very mixed freight.

J. G. Dewing

Plate 218 (above): A Manchester to Aberystwyth Easter Monday excursion is pictured near Abermule on 10th April 1939, headed by 'Dukedog' No. 3222, which later became No. 9022. Note the wide variety of coaching stock, including two clerestories.

J. G. Dewing

Plate 219 (below): A formidable task lies ahead for this Dean 3252 class 'Duke', with its eight coach excursion from Birmingham to the Cambrian Coast on 9th April 1939, as it leaves Abermule in fine style, with the climb to Talerddig Summit ahead. The locomotive is No. 3284 *Isle of Jersey* which was built in 1899.

J. G. Dewing

Plate 220 (above): 'Dukedog' No. 3202 (later No. 9002) when less than three years old, is seen carrying out one of the duties for which the class was specifically built, namely passenger traffic on the Cambrian lines. It was photographed on 10th April 1939, climbing to Talerddig Summit with a local passenger train.

J. G. Dewing

Plate 221 (below): An Aberystwyth to Whitchurch train, with some vintage rolling stock, leaves Carno on 18th July 1938 headed by 'Dukedog' No. 3211 (later No. 9011).

J. G. Dewing

Plate 222 (right): This little Hunslet Engine Co. 0-6-0T, No. 819, built in 1903, had an interesting life. It was absorbed by the Cambrian Railways in 1904 from the Lambourne Valley Railway, and then into GWR stock in 1922. It was originally named *Eadweade.* The original Hunslet chimney was replaced by Swindon in 1938, and the locomotive is seen on 10th April 1939 at Moat Lane Junction. It was the only member of the class and was withdrawn in 1946.

J. G. Dewing

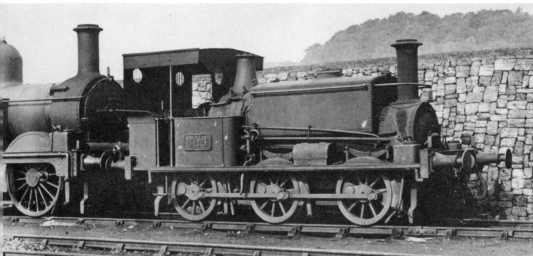

Plate 223 (left): On 14th September 1937, Oswestry Depot had Manning Wardle 0-6-0ST No. 824 on shed. This locomotive, built in 1865 and acquired by the Cambrian Railways from the Mawddwy Railway in 1911, survived until 1940.

J. G. Dewing

Plate 224 (below): This delightful little 2-4-0T tank engine, No. 1308 *Lady Margaret,* joined the Cambrian Railways from the Liskeard & Looe Railway in 1922. It was built in 1902 and survived until 1948. This scene was photographed on 14th September 1937, at Oswestry Station.

J. G. Dewing

Plate 225 (left): Sharp, Stewart & Co. 0-6-0 No. 900, built in 1864, is seen at Oswestry Shed on 14th September 1937. Twenty two of these locomotives were built, the first being withdrawn in 1899 and the last in 1947.

J. G. Dewing

Plate 226 (right): Three of these Sharp, Stewart 2-4-0Ts were built for the Cambrian Railways in 1866. They were all rebuilt at Swindon in 1922, and in 1927, No. 1192 went to the Hemyock branch and was scrapped in 1929. The other two lasted until 1948 at Oswestry, and both achieved a remarkable million miles in service. No. 1196 is pictured at Oswestry on the Tanat Valley Light Railway train to Llangynog on 11th September 1935.

J. G. Dewing

Plate 227 (below): A 'Dukedog' and 'Duke' are pictured double-heading near Commins Coch on 18th July 1938, with the 1p.m. Aberystwyth to Paddington express. 'Dukedog' No. 3204 (later No. 9004) is piloting 'Duke' No. 3268 *Chough* (note the variation in chimneys).

J. G. Dewing

Plate 228 (right): The 2.05p.m. Whitchurch to Aberystwyth train is seen near Carno headed by 'Dukedog' No. 3213 (later No. 9013) on 18th July 1938. These rather old-fashioned looking locomotives do not look as if they were built as late as 1936 to 1939. They were extremely successful and operated over the Cambrian lines for over twenty years. Happily, No. 9017 is preserved.

J. G. Dewing

Plate 229 (below): A train for Shrewsbury is pictured shortly after leaving Welshpool, on 19th July 1938. It is headed by one of the 156 'Bulldog' class locomotives, No. 3437, which was one of the few members of the class never to carry a name. Parts from 29 of these locomotives were used in the construction of the 'Dukedogs'.

J. G. Dewing

Plate 230 (left): One of the 156 3300 'Bulldog' class double-framed locomotives, No. 340: *Empire of India*, waits at Wolverhampton (Low Level) on 2nd June 1936. Many members of the class had their names removed in the 1920s and early 1930s. They were built between 1889 and 1910, the last one being withdrawn in 1951.

J. P. Wilson

Plate 231 (right): Another member of the 'Bulldog' class, No. 3378 *River Tawe*, is pictured at Bristol on 5th June 1938. The name was removed in 1939.

J. P. Wilson

Plate 232 (left): On 11th July 1925, No. 3715 *City of Hereford*, a member of the famous 3700 'City' class passes Chipping Campden with an 'up' Worcester to Paddington express. There were twenty locomotives in the class, and No. 3717 *City of Truro* was preserved, after withdrawal in 1931, after its historic run down Wellington Bank in 1904, when a speed of 102.3m.p.h. was claimed.

H. G. W. Household

Plate 233 (right): A 3252 'Duke of Cornwall' class locomotive, No. 3290 *Severn* is seen, on 7th April 1936, at Oswestry. Sixty of these fine locomotives were built between 1895 and 1899, the last to be withdrawn being as late as 1951.

J. G. Dewing

Plate 234 (right): A 4120 'Atbara' class locomotive, No. 4133 *Roberts*, hauls a Cardiff to Gloucester slow passenger train in October 1924. The class consisted of thirty locomotives, all being withdrawn by 1931 after only twenty years of service.

H. G. W. Household

Plate 235 (left): No. 4161 *Hyacianth* hauls a Wolverhampton to Weston-super-Mare train near Hatherley Junction, Cheltenham, on 9th July 1924. At one time the name carried an 'E' at the end (*Hyacianthe*).

H. G. W. Household

Plate 236 (right): The Dean 3521 class had an interesting career. No. 3525, seen in this view, started as a 0-4-2T in 1887, and was rebuilt between 1891 and 1892 as an 0-4-4T. Further rebuilding to a 4-4-0 took place between 1899 and 1902. The locomotive, looking rather dirty for the period, is seen near Charlton Kings, Cheltenham, on 5th July 1924, with through coaches from Paddington, which it had hauled from Kingham.

H. G. W. Household

Plate 237 (left): No. 3204, one o[f] the twenty 'Barnum' 3206 class 2-4-0s simmers at Wellington Shed on 28t[h] April 1922. These little locomotives ha[d] the longest careers of the Dean 2-4-0s the first one being built in 1889, and th[e] last one being withdrawn 48 years later in 1937.

H. G. W. Househol[d]

Plate 238 (right): One of the eighty one 2600 class 2-6-0 'Aberdares', No. 2629, heads a freight from Bordesley near Hatherley Junction, Cheltenham, on 24th September 1924.

H. G. W. Household

Plate 239 (below): Two hundred and sixty of the 2301 class 'Dean Goods' 0-6-0s were built between 1883 and 1899. No less than 54 passed into British Railways' ownership, the last one being withdrawn in 1957. Many saw service overseas in both world wars. Most returned from World War I, but many were lost during World War II in France. No. 2566 is seen leaving Didcot on 10th June 1939, with a train for the Didcot, Newbury & Southampton line.

J. G. Dewing

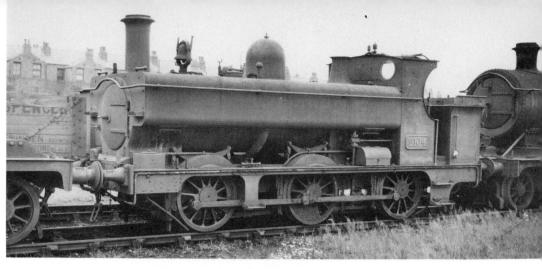

Plate 240 (right): No. 2104, one of the 140 class 2021 0-6-0PTs, is seen on 5th August 1947 at Tyseley Shed, Birmingham. Note the bell fitted above the boiler; this was a feature of the locomotives allocated to Birkenhead for working in the docks. The locomotive was originally built with a domeless boiler, but No. 2104 had since acquired a standard domed version.

J. P. Wilson

Plate 241 (left): A class 455 'Metropolitan' tank, No. 3585, was on Oxford Depot on 17th June 1938. One hundred and forty were built between 1869 and 1899. This locomotive, at this date, was not fitted with condensing apparatus. The last one to be withdrawn was in 1949, which was, in fact, 51 years after the first withdrawal.

J. G. Dewing

Plate 242 (right): An 850 class saddle tank, No. 1925, stands on Didcot Depot on 28th September 1936. It was built in 1884, the class consisting of 170 locomotives, 43 passing into British Railways' ownership, and most being altered to pannier tanks during their careers.

J. G. Dewing

Plate 243 (below): A pannier conversion of the 850 class seen in *Plate 242.* No. 1902, converted in December 1927, is ready to leave Cirencester Town on 19th September 1937. The locomotive was withdrawn in 1943.

J. G. Dewing

Plate 244 (left): An immaculate Worcester based 'Castle', No. 7013 *Bristol Castle*, restarts the 'up' 'Cathedrals Express' from an out of course signal check at Port Meadow, on the approach to Oxford, on 6th July 1962. This locomotive was, in fact, the original No. 4082 *Windsor Castle* (*see Plate 62*).

R. Leslie

Plate 245 (below): Storm clouds seem to be brewing around the coast at Teignmouth as 'Castle' No. 5071 *Spitfire* blows off just at the right moment for the photographer, as it heads the 'down' 'Cornishman' along the sea wall on 19th July 1956. This locomotive was originally named *Clifford Castle* but altered in September 1940. The name *Clifford Castle* was ultimately carried by 'Castle' No. 5098.

R. C. Riley

Plate 246 (right): Nearly at its journey's end is the 'down' 'Devonian', seen leaving Teignmouth on 17th July 1958, headed by Newton Abbot 'Castle' No. 4083 *Abbotsbury Castle.* This train, often loaded to fourteen or fifteen coaches, started at Bradford (Forster Square) and travelled via Leeds, Birmingham (New Street), and Bristol (Temple Meads) to its destination at Paignton.

R. C. Riley

Plate 247 (below): The little girl on platform 3 at Paddington seems totally absorbed by the magnificent spectacle of immaculate Old Oak Common 'Castle' No. 7024 *Powis Castle*, ready to leave on the last steam-hauled 'down' 'Bristolian' on the morning of 12th June 1959.

J. D. Edwards

Plate 248 (right): The driver of single-sleeved chimney 'King', No. 6003 *King George IV*, appears to be rather anxious about something, after its arrival at Wolverhampton (Low Level) with the 'down' 'Inter-City' on 21st July 1954. The train was the 9a.m. from Paddington.

B. Morrison

Plate 249 (below): On 28th March 1959, the Pwllheli portion of the 'up' 'Cambrian Coast Express' runs along the banks of the Dovey Estuary, between Aberdovey and Dovey Junction, where it will be attached to the portion from Aberystwyth before heading for Shrewsbury with a 'Manor' class locomotive. Machynlleth Shed kept locomotives well groomed for this working, as is evident from the condition of 2-6-2T No. 5541 in the fully lined green livery.

Gavin Morrison

Plate 250 (right): The 'down' 'Torbay Express' heads rapidly along the level track as it approaches Twyford on 5th July 1951. The locomotive is Newton Abbot-based 'Castle' No. 5011 *Tintagel Castle.*

B. Morrison

Plate 251 (below): The 'up' 'Cambrian Coast Express', headed by an immaculate 'King', No. 6002 *King William IV*, approaches King's Sutton, just north of Aynho Junction, on 23rd June 1961.

R. Leslie

Focus on Paddington

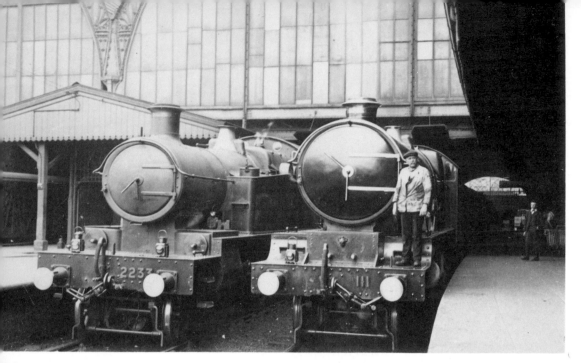

Plate 252 (left): The driver of the famous Great Western Pacific No. 111 *The Great Bear* poses on the running plate before leaving with an express for Bristol, whilst on the left, 'County' tank No. 2233 is ready to depart with a train from Paddington for the outer suburbs, a duty for which they were specifically designed.

OPC Collection

Plate 253 (below left): The name board of the 'Cheltenham Spa Express' lies on the running plate of 'Castle' No. 7000 *Viscount Portal* after its arrival at platform 9 Paddington, whilst on platform 10 double chimney 'Castle' No. 5061 *Earl of Birkenhead* has arrived with the 'up' 'Capitals United Express', in April 1961.

J. B. Snell

Plate 254 (above): The 2.15p.m express for Cheltenham is ready to leave platform 3 at Paddington headed by immaculate Gloucester based 'Castle' No. 5018 *St. Mawes Castle,* in 1952.

M. W. Earley

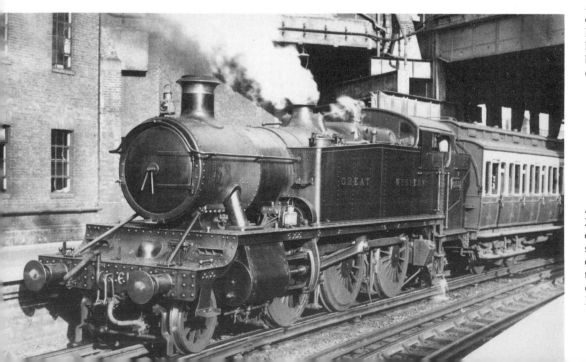

Plate 255 (left): The 6100 class 2-6-2Ts were specifically built in the early 1930s for the London suburban services, and continued on these duties until ousted by diesel multiple units in the 1960s. A member of the class awaits departure from Paddington in October 1933.

J. G. Dewing

Plate 256 (right): One of the eleven condensing 0-6-0 pannier tanks, No. 9703, performs empty carriage shunting duties at Paddington on 4th July 1959. These locomotives were always shedded at Old Oak Common Depot for their duties on the Metropolitan lines.

C. R. L. Coles

Plate 257 (below): A fine picture of No. 1027 County of Stafford, making a spirited departure from Paddington with a 'down' express for Bristol (Temple Meads) on 27th August 1960. The locomotive is fitted with the ugly double chimney and new double blastpipe, which did little for the appearance but gave an improvement in performance and efficiency.

R. C. Riley

Focus on Bristo

Plate 258 (left): A bird's-eye view of No. 6832 *Brockton Grange* leaving Bristol (Temple Meads) on 2nd June 1962, with a train for Weston-super-Mare.

John Whiteley

Plate 259 (below): An immaculate 'Castle' has been turned out for the last steam-hauled 'up' 'Bristolian' on 12th June 1959. No. 5085 *Evesham Abbey* had been given the honour, and judging by the number of people on the platform, it looks like being a full train.

J. D. Edwards

Plate 260 (above): A 'Castle' class locomotive, No. 5071 *Spitfire*, fitted with a double chimney, pulls into Bristol (Temple Meads) at the head of an 'up' Liverpool to Plymouth express on 2nd June 1963.

John Whiteley

Plate 261 (below): An interesting view showing a train to Portishead passing beneath Clifton Suspension Bridge over the Avon Gorge, headed by a Class 4500 2-6-2T on 5th June 1938.

J. P. Wilson

Plate 262 (above): On 13th May 1952, two immaculate Cardiff (Canton) 'Castles', Nos. 5007 *Rougemont Castle* and 4094 *Dynevor Castle*, prepare to change over on the 'up' 'Red Dragon' express to Paddington, at Cardiff (General) Station. Note the two different types of chimneys fitted to the locomotives.

R. C. Riley

Plate 263 (below): A picture which was typical of the Welsh Valleys for many years shows a Cameron Taff Vale Railway A class 0-6-2T, No. 312, which was rebuilt with a Swindon taper boiler between 1924 and 1932, entering Pontypridd on 13th May 1952, with 'British Railways' painted on the tank sides.

R. C. Riley

Plate 264 (right): No. 7828 *Odney Manor* was only seventeen months old when this picture was taken on 15th May 1952. It is on an 'up' freight passing Cardiff (Canton) Depot. The locomotive is in the lined black British Railways livery, and had been parted from the normal standard Churchward 3,500 gallon tender, and connected to an 'intermediate' 3,500 gallon type with long side fenders.

R. C. Riley

Plate 265 (left): A recently ex-works 2-8-2T No. 7240, heads a rake of empty coal wagons from Radyr on 12th May 1952, and is pictured passing Penrhos Junction on its journey up the valley.

R. C. Riley

Plate 266 (right): Ex-Rhymney Railway Harry Riches A class 0-6-2T No. 59, built in 1909, is seen shortly after an overhaul at Caerphilly Works, working a freight near Heath Junction, north of Cardiff on the Rhymney line, in 1952.

R. C. Riley

Freight around the Great Western Lines

Plate 267 (above): One of the 260 Dean 2301 class locomotives, No. 2395, is seen on 4th May 1940, heading an 'up' goods near Gerrards Cross on the Great Western & Great Central Joint line. Note the immaculate state of the cutting sides, compared with the 1980s.

J. G. Dewing

Plate 268 (below): One of the Class 3000 Robinson (Great Central Railway) 2-8-0s, purchased by the GWR from the Railway Operating Division of the Royal Engineers (ROD), is seen in British Railways livery passing Kennington Junction, Oxford with an 'up' freight, on 30th August 1953. Eighty two of these locomotives were purchased by the GWR, the last one working until 1958.

L. Elsey

Plate 269 (above): Most 4200 class 2-8-0Ts were based in South Wales, but a few were allocated to St. Blazey Shed in Cornwall for the china clay traffic. No. 4247 heads empty china clay wagons near Par on 8th July 1955.

R. C. Riley

Plate 270 (below): The wartime dirt is well and truly encrusted on 'Saint' class locomotive No. 2906 Lady of Lynn, as it heads a train of milk empties past Reading (West) Junction in 1943. Note the ARP curtain over the cab roof, and the signals which are positively black with grime.

M. W. Earley

Plate 271 (left): Ex-Swansea Harbour Trust 0-4-0ST No. 1142 (*see Plate 205*) shunts at Clee Hill Summit before leaving for Bitterly with chippings from Titterstone Quarry on 15th August 1958.

B. Morrison

Plate 272 (below): It was an unusual sight, in 1955, to see a Class 6100 2-6-2T on freight. No. 6101 is seen on a 'down' goods from Slough to Reading (West) Junction, in Sonning Cutting, in April 1955.

M. W. Earley

Plate 273 (right): No. 5818, which was one of the twenty locomotives of the 4800 class 0-4-2Ts built without auto-train gear and ATC apparatus, shunts at Abingdon on 28th July 1959. The locomotive was built in 1933, which is much later than its appearance would suggest.

J. D. Edwards

Plate 274 (below): No. 2894 was one of the 2-8-0s of the 2800 class fitted with side window cabs. It is on an 'H' class freight crossing over from the goods lines behind Reading Station to the 'up' main line at East Main box in 1949. This batch of the class was usually known as the 2884s.

M. W. Earley

Plate 275 (above): Displaced from passenger duties by diesel multiple units, 6100 class 2-6-2T No. 6136 of Slough leaves Hinksey Yard, south of Oxford, with an 'up' freight on 4th March 1960.

J. D. Edwards

Plate 276 (above): An Oxford-based 7200 class, No. 7218, leaves Hinksey Yard, Oxford, with a freight from Morris Cowley on 4th March 1960. This locomotive was a rebuild of 4200 class 2-8-2T No. 5293, which was one of the batch of twenty which was stored when originally built in October 1930 until being rebuilt in November 1934.

J. D. Edwards

Plate 277 (right): A 4300 class Mogul, No. 6326, passes Kennington Junction, Oxford, with a special train of BMC products for the Scottish Motor Show on 6th November 1959.

J. D. Edwards

Plate 278 (below): A recent ex-works 2-8-0 of the 2884 class, built as late as 1939, is seen at Hinksey South with a 'down' freight for Oxford on 15th August 1959.

J. D. Edwards

Double-Heading around the Great Western

Plate 279 (right): Llangollen Station is the setting for this picture of 0-6-0PT No. 9669, helping out an unidentified 'Manor' on a summer Saturdays only train from Butlin's, on the Cambrian Coast, for Manchester. It was photographed in August 1954, before most of the 'Manor' class had been given the improved draughting.

J. B. Snell

Plate 280 (below): On the last day of service on the Cardigan branch, an unusual double-heading occurred using two Class 4500 2-6-2Ts, Nos. 4569 and 4557, pictured leaving Boncarth on 8th September 1962.

Gavin Morrison

Plate 281 (left): One of the early batch of 'Halls', No. 4915 *Condover Hall*, pilot No. 1012 *County of Denbigh* away from Newton Abbot, past Aller Junction, prior to the formidable climb to Dainton Summit on 16th July 1955. Both locomotives are running in the British Railways lined black livery.

L. Elsey

Plate 282 (right): Assistance is given to 'Castle' class locomotive No. 5049 *Earl of Plymouth* by 'Grange' No. 6873 *Caradoc Grange* up Wrangton Bank, west of Brent, on 21st June 1958.

L. Elsey

Plate 283 (below): A summer Saturdays only train from Ilfracombe to Wolverhampton climbs Wilmcote Bank, on 22nd August 1964, headed by an unidentified 'Hall' and Mogul No. 6364. The Mogul would have been attached at Stratford-upon-Avon.

J. R. P. Hunt

Plate 284 (right): Power at the head of this 'down' express on Rattery Bank is being provided by No. 6907 *Davenham Hall* and No. 6003 *King George IV* on 20th August 1949. Note the absence of the crest on the tender of No. 6907, which is in lined black livery.

J. G. Dewing

Plate 285 (left): On 20th August 1949, No. 6907 *Davenham Hall* was rostered for piloting duties over the South Devon banks. It is pictured assisting No. 6022 *King Edward III* with an 'up' express on Hemerdon Bank.

J. G. Dewing

Plate 286 (right): A 4300 class Mogul, No. 7310, pilots 2251 class 0-6-0 No. 2209 away from Ruabon with a 'down' Barmouth express on 9th August 1956.

B. Morrison

Plate 287 (above): On 6th July 1957, a heavy 'up' summer Saturdays extra needs double-heading on the easier gradients, east of Exeter. No. 5999 *Wollaton Hall* is giving assistance to No. 6830 *Buckenhill Grange* as the train passes Stoke Cannon, which was the junction for the Exe Valley line to Tiverton.   *R. C. Riley*

Plate 288 (below): The external state of these locomotives is not what one would have expected for such a prestigious train as the 'down' 'Cornish Riviera Express'. On summer Saturdays, in the mid-1950s, the 'King' class locomotive was detached at Newton Abbot as the train ran fast to Truro and 'Kings' were banned west of Plymouth. No. 6855 *Saighton Grange* and 'Modified Hall' No. 6988 *Swithland Hall* blast their way past Stoneycombe Quarry, on the 1 in 46 section of the climb to Dainton Summit, on 19th July 1958.

R. C. Riley

Diesel Railcars

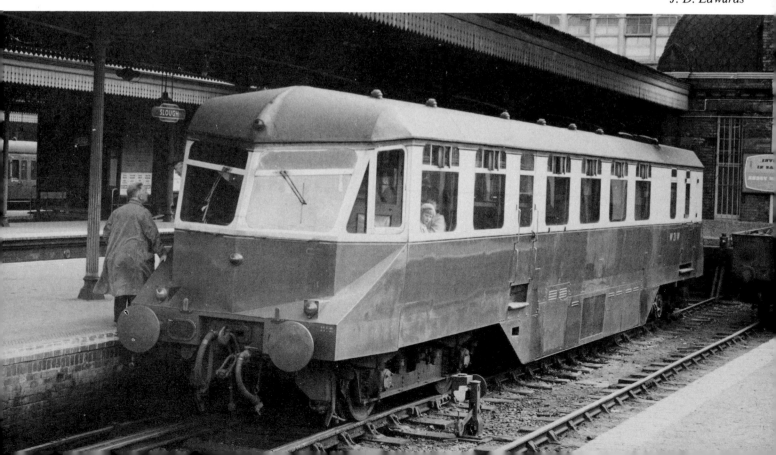

Plate 289 (above): The Great Western introduced diesel rail-cars in 1934. There were two basic designs as shown on this page. Nos. 1-16 were like No. 4, seen here at Swindon on 18th March 1960. This railcar, together with Nos. 2 and 3, had buffet facilities, and was used between Birmingham and Cardiff. Happily No. 4 has been preserved; the bodywork was by Park Royal Ltd. and the builder was AEC.

J. D. Edwards

Plate 290 (below): On 19th April 1958, No. W21W waits in the bay platform at Slough with the Windsor branch service. It was one of the batch of twenty built between 1940 and 1942. These units had AEC engines and were constructed at Swindon. They were fitted with standard buffers and drawgear for hauling up to 60 tons. A speed of 40m.p.h. was the maximum for No. W21W. No. 17 and 34 were parcels cars and Nos. 35 to 38 were twin units.

J. D. Edwards

Plate 291 (above): One of the two 2ft. 6in. gauge Beyer Peacock 0-6-0Ts, built in 1902, is No. 822 *The Earl*, seen without its nameplate. It has just arrived at Welshpool with a freight on 10th August 1956, which was the year that the line was closed by British Railways.

B. Morrison

Plate 292 (above): The other locomotive on the line was numbered 823 by the GWR, and named *Countess*. It is pictured resplendent in its GWR livery on 12th September 1935.

J. G. Dewing

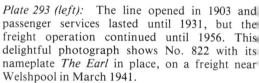

The Narrow Gauge

The Welshpool & Llanfair Railway

Plate 293 (left): The line opened in 1903 and passenger services lasted until 1931, but the freight operation continued until 1956. This delightful photograph shows No. 822 with its nameplate *The Earl* in place, on a freight near Welshpool in March 1941.

J. G. Dewing

Plate 294 (right): The end came for the line in 1956, and the future for the locomotives looked bleak. Instead of being cut up they were stored in Oswestry Works until 1961/2, when they were sold to The Welshpool & Llanfair Light Railway Preservation Society. The two locomotives are pictured inside the works on 21st June 1958.

Gavin Morrison

Plate 295 (right): On 30th May 1964, the Vale of Rheidol Railway had a busy day, as the Gainsborough Model Railway Society arrived with a nine coach special at Aberystwyth for a trip on the line. Locomotives No. 8 *Llywelyn* and No. 9 *Prince of Wales* were rostered, both, at this time, running in the smart lined Brunswick green livery of British Railways. Note the 6F shed plate on No. 8, showing that the line was now under the control of the Midland Region of British Railways.

Gavin Morrison

The Vale of Rheidol Railway

Plate 296 (right): The line was opened in 1902 and Davies & Metcalf built two 2-6-2Ts of 1ft. 11½in. gauge, these being numbered 1 and 2, becoming 1212 and 1213. It is sometimes overlooked that the line has had four locomotives built for it, the two already mentioned plus two more built by Swindon in 1923. No 1212 was withdrawn in 1932, but No. 1213, which became No. 9 in 1946, is seen here, bearing the name *Prince of Wales*, en route to Devil's Bridge on 8th September 1962.

Gavin Morrison

Plate 297 (right): No. 9 *Prince of Wales* is seen again on 8th September 1962, running round the coaching stock at Devil's Bridge. Happily, British Railways have continued to run this spectacular line, but the liveries of locomotives and stock have seen many changes. Other major changes to the line have been the alteration of the departure point, bringing it into Aberystwyth's BR station, and the closing of the old shed. The locomotives now use the former standard gauge depot.

G. W. Morrison

Plate 298 (left): One of the splendid 6100 class 2-6-2Ts, No. 6104, in unlined black livery, heads a local train away from Reading West on 29th June 1957.

L. Elsey

Plate 299 (below): Newton Abbot-based 5100 class 2-6-2T, No. 4117, departs from Exeter (St. David's) with a 'down' local train on 31st August 1956. This locomotive was one of a batch of twenty built in 1935 and 1936. The large 2-6-2Ts, with variations, were built over a period of 46 years, from 1903 to 1949.

P. H. Groom

Plate 300 (right): This is what one might describe as a typical Great Western London commuter train of the 1930s. A 6100 class 2-6-2T, No. 6102, works the 5.05p.m. Paddington to Hungerford train, near Southcote Junction, in 1939. This train was rostered to leave Paddington with ten coaches, of which two were slipped at Taplow, four coaches left at Reading for Oxford, leaving four for the final stretch to Hungerford, plus, in this case, a 'Dreadnought' third. What a splendid way to commute to and from work!

M. W. Earley

Plate 301 (left): A Gloucester-based 4575 class 2-6-2T, No. 5514, runs round the stock of the 4p.m. train from Kingham, at Chipping Norton, on 7th June 1958. At this time, the line was truncated in the tunnel as a head shunt, but formerly ran through to Banbury.

J. D. Edwards

Plate 302 (right): 5100 class 2-6-2T No. 5196 awaits departure from Birmingham (Snow Hill) with the 3.55p.m. train to Stourbridge Junction on 5th August 1947. These locomotives worked the suburban trains around Brimingham and Wolverhampton for around 25 years or more, until displaced by diesel multiple units in the mid-1960s.

J. P. Wilson

LEAMINGTON

Plate 303 (above): The train arrangements board at Leamington, on 9th May 1965, captures the atmosphere of the steam shed signing-on area.   *J. R. P. Hunt*

Plate 304 (above): A 2-6-2T, No. 4178, simmers gently on Leamington Shed, on 29th March 1964, while Nos. 4133 and 4151 appear to be not in steam.   *J. R. P. Hunt*

Plate 305 (below): On a Sunday in September 1962, two of Carmarthen's 'Castles' are seen on the depot waiting to be steamed for the following week's duties. They are No. 4081 *Warwick Castle* and No. 5087 *Tintern Abbey*.

Gavin Morrison

CARMARTHEN

WORCESTER WORKS

Plate 306 (right): An interesting picture, taken in Worcester Works on 18th April 1964. The locomotives from the rear are No. 5054 *Earl of Ducie*, No. 4920 *Dumbleton Hall*, now preserved on the Dart Valley Railway and undergoing restoration, and No. 6873 *Caradoc Grange*. By this time, it is doubtful if some of the locomotives ever re-entered traffic.

J. R. P. Hunt

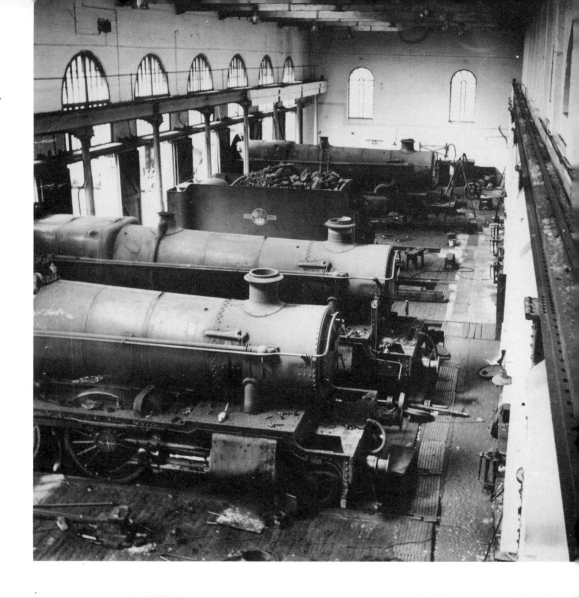

Plate 307 (below): Lined up at Cardiff (Canton) Depot on 2nd June 1962, are No. 4080 *Powderham Castle*, No. 6010 *King Charles I*, being prepared for a train to Shrewsbury, No. 7913 *Little Wyrley Hall* and 2-8-0 No. 3803. Only a few 'Kings' were allocated to Cardiff (Canton) and then only for a short time around 1961/2. No. 6010, and others, were withdrawn during June 1962.

Gavin Morrison

CARDIFF (CANTON)

LLANELLY

Plate 308 (left): On 12th August 1963, Llanelly Depot does not seem to be very full. Present on this occasion are a 'Castle' in the background, a group of 2-8-0Ts, and one of the small 2-6-2Ts of the 4575 class, No. 5554.

J. R. P. Hunt

SWINDON

Plate 309 (below): Some of the finest roundhouse sheds in the country were to be found on the Great Western, with Swindon being one of the most impressive, as it could be relied upon to produce fine line-ups. On 2nd September 1956, an unidentified 'Modified Hall' was present with No. 5000 *Launceston Castle*, No. 5009 *Shrewsbury Castle*, No. 6023 *King Edward II*, not long before being fitted with the double chimney, and 2-8-0 No. 3836.

Gavin Morrison

Great Western Miscellany

Plate 310 (right): No. 102 *La France* was the first of the three 'De Glehn' Compound Atlantic locomotives, which G. J. Churchward ordered from the Société Alsacienne des Constructions Méchaniques in 1903. The locomotive was assembled at Swindon, and it was an impressive machine. It was rebuilt with a Swindon taper boiler in 1916, and remained in traffic until 1926.
OPC Collection

Plate 311 (left): No. 1364 was one of the five Churchward-built 0-6-0Ts of the 1361 class built in 1910. It is pictured in ex-works condition at Plymouth Docks on 12th July 1955. The very short wheelbase allowed the class to operate the sharp curves around the docks. They were, in fact, of a non-standard GWR design by Holcroft.
R. C. Riley

Plate 312 (right): One of the nine Midland & South Western Junction Railway Tyrrell 4-4-0s, No. 1126, built between 1905 and 1914, is seen at Worcester about 1937. This locomotive was rebuilt, along with five others in the class, with Swindon taper boilers, during the period from 1924 to 1929.
J. G. Dewing

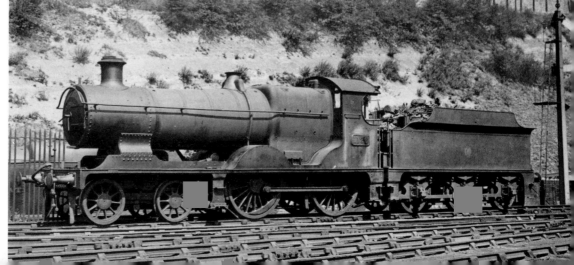

Plate 313 (above): Looking very smart in the British Railways lined green livery is 5100 class 2-6-2T No. 4111, lined up at the coaling stage at Tyseley on 16th June 1957.

Gavin Morrison

Plate 314 (above): A 'Saint' class 4-6-0, No. 2933 *Bibury Court*, performs mundane duties whilst working out its last few months. It prepares to leave Shrewsbury with the 4.50p.m. train to Gobowen on 28th August 1952.

B. Morrison

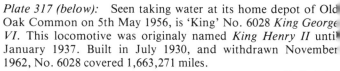

Plate 315 (left): 'Modified Hall' No. 7924 *Thornycroft Hall* stands on Westbury Depot on 25th February 1962. The locomotive was built as late as September 1950.

Gavin Morrison

Plate 316 (below): The first of the 1923 batch of the 4200 class 2-8-0Ts was No. 5205, photographed on Gloucester Shed on 20th August 1964. This was the first locomotive of the class to be built with outside steam pipes and the increased cylinder diameter of 19in.

Gavin Morrison

Plate 317 (below): Seen taking water at its home depot of Old Oak Common on 5th May 1956, is 'King' No. 6028 *King George VI*. This locomotive was originaly named *King Henry II* until January 1937. Built in July 1930, and withdrawn November 1962, No. 6028 covered 1,663,271 miles.

R. C. Riley

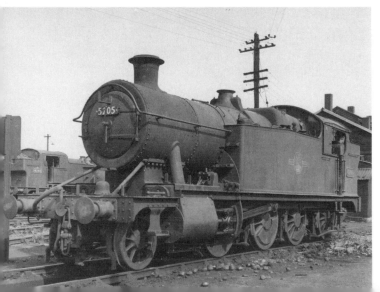

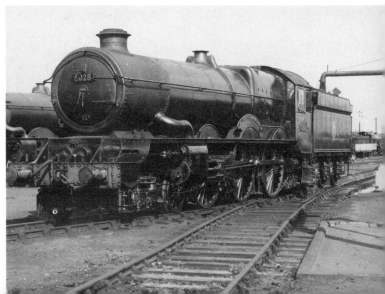

Plate 318 (right): Together at Southall Shed, on 14th October 1962, are No. 7923 *Speke Hall* and 6100 class 2-6-2T No. 6133. Both locomotives look quite well-kept considering steam was rapidly being run down in this area at the time.

Gavin Morrison

Plate 319 (left): 'Grange' class locomotive, No. 6824 *Ashley Grange*, makes a fine sight as it pulls away from Oxford on 13th July 1963, with the 'down' 5.15p.m. Paddington to Worcester express. This train was formerly the 'down' 'Cathedrals Express'.

R. Leslie

Plate 320 (right): The end has come for 'County' Class No. 1014 *County of Glamorgan*, as it lies cold and lifeless at the back of Swindon waiting to be cut up. Note the wooden numberplates and, presumably, the nameplate as well, as it was the only locomotive to have the name left on it in the dump on 26th April 1964.

Gavin Morrison

Plate 321 (left): Heavy work for 5100 class 2-6-2T No. 5167, as it approaches King's Sutton with an 'up' freight of sixty wagons from Banbury to Oxford on 23rd June 1961.

R. Leslie

Plate 322 (below): Carmarthen-based 'Castle' No. 5054 *Earl of Ducie* has just returned from its last overhaul at Swindon, and is seen at its home depot on 9th September 1962, looking immaculate and well-loaded with coal. This locomotive worked the Bristol to Paddington leg of the famous high speed railtour to Plymouth on 9th May 1964, achieving a speed well into the upper nineties.

Gavin Morrison

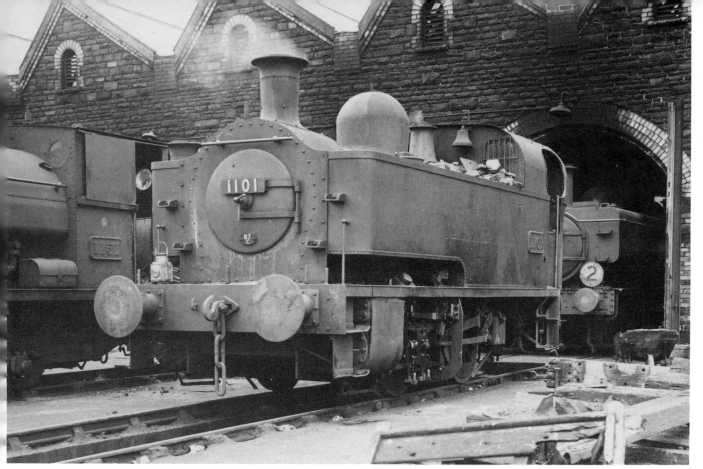

Plate 323 (above): The Great Western only ever built one class of 0-4-0Ts, although they owned many which were absorbed from other lines. The 1101 class consisted of six locomotives, built in 1926 by the Avonside Engine Co. They were to replace older 0-4-0Ts from the absorbed Swansea Harbour Trust. All locomotives were allocated to Danygraig, at Swansea, where No. 1101 is seen in August 1957. *J. D. Edwards*

Plate 324 (below): A fine study of the recently ex-works 7200 class 2-8-2T No. 7213, at Gloucester Shed on 22nd June 1952. This loco-motive was rebuilt in 1934 from one of the Class 5205 2-8-0Ts, which were stored after building and never entered service. *L. Elsey*

Plate 325 (above): Fresh from its last major overhaul, 'King' No. 6011 *King James I* stands beside Westbury Shed on 25th February 1962. It is hard to believe that ten months later it was withdrawn from service, and scrapped at Swindon, after covering 1,718,295 miles in 34 years of service.

Gavin Morrison

Plate 326 (below): The last 'Castle' to be built, in August 1950, was No. 7037, appropriately named *Swindon*, and it is pictured on Neath Shed on 3rd June 1962. Nine months later it was withdrawn, having given only thirteen years service, covering 519,885 miles.

Gavin Morrison